P9-EEK-024

Easy
PAPER-PIECED
MINIATURES

Carol Doak

That Patchwork Place®

An imprint of Martingale & Company

Dedication

This book is dedicated to Rita Rehm, the workshop student who first motivated me to explore miniature paper piecing. Although Rita inspired this journey, she represents many delightful students. They often encourage a design direction and a quest for an easier way to accomplish a goal. They are the wind beneath my wings.

Acknowledgments

My heartfelt thanks and appreciation go to:

Terry Maddox for her wonderful Flying Nuns quilt. Where I saw little Rain Bonnet Sues, she imagined nuns, and carried her concept through beautifully.

Ginny Guaraldi, for her delightful presentation of the Simply Spools quilt and for sharing her neat machine-quilting tip.

Sherry Reis, for making the Tree of Life quilt into a special Christmas celebration and for always being there with hugs, whether in person or through the phone.

To everyone at That Patchwork Place who contributed their expertise and shared their friendship during the process of bringing together an idea.

And finally, to Ursula Reikes, for her friendship and wonderful technical editing, and for making writing this book so much fun!

MISSION STATEMENT

We are dedicated to providing quality products and service by working together to inspire creativity and to enrich the lives we touch.

Credits

Editor-in-Chief	Kerry I. Smith
Technical Editor	Ursula Reikes
Managing Editor	Judy Petry
Copy Editor	Tina Cook
Proofreader	Leslie Phillips
Design Director	Cheryl Stevenson
Cover Designer	Lisa McKenney
Text Designer	Kay Green
Design Assistant	Marijane E. Figg
Illustrator	Laurel Strand
Photographer	Brent Kane

Easy Paper-Pieced Miniatures
© 1998 by Carol Doak

Martingale & Company
PO Box 118
Bothell, WA 98041-0118 USA

No part of this product may be reproduced in any form, unless otherwise stated, in which case reproduction is limited to the use of the purchaser. The written instructions, photographs, designs, projects, and patterns are intended for the personal, noncommercial use of the retail purchaser and are under federal copyright laws; they are not to be reproduced by any electronic, mechanical, or other means, including informational storage or retrieval systems, for commercial use.

The information in this book is presented in good faith, but no warranty is given nor results guaranteed. Since Martingale & Company has no control over choice of materials or procedures, the company assumes no responsibility for the use of this information.

Printed in Canada
03 02 01 00 99 98   6 5 4 3

Library of Congress Cataloging-in-Publication Data
Doak, Carol.
   Easy paper-pieced miniatures / Carol Doak.
      p. cm.
   ISBN 1-56477-209-8
      1. Patchwork—Patterns. 2. Quilting. 3. Miniature quilts.
   I. Title.
TT835.D628 1998
746.46'041—dc21   97-48430
                                                          CIP

TABLE OF CONTENTS

PREFACE

So, exactly what is machine paper piecing and why would you use this technique to make miniature quilts, even if you have never made a miniature quilt? To paper piece, you cut oversize fabric pieces and sew them to a paper foundation, following a numbered design. The accuracy of this technique allows you to create miniature patchwork that you would never dream of attempting with traditional piecing methods. And because paper piecing is a method rather than an acquired skill, beginners and experienced quilters can create accurate patchwork blocks right from the start.

Although I knew that machine paper piecing produced accurate small pieces and sharp points, I never considered exactly how small the patchwork could be until I received a 1" x 1" Basket-block pin from a workshop student. She used a 1" x 1" block-front drawing from my book *Easy Machine Paper Piecing* to create a smaller version of a 4" patchwork block. My first reaction was amazement and my second reaction was intrigue.

I thought, why not? Paper piecing is the perfect way to create miniature patchwork quilts.

◆ Sewing miniature patchwork isn't any more difficult than sewing full-size patchwork—you just stitch shorter seams.

◆ Cutting fabric is easy, because a cut shape of one size can be used for patches of several sizes.

◆ Ignoring fabric grain is fine, because the grain isn't noticeable in the tiny patches.

◆ Stitching is easy, because although you finish with tiny patches, you stitch oversized pieces onto a foundation, then trim.

I first experimented with the block-front drawings from my book *Easy Reversible Vests*. These designs are a bit larger than 1" x 1". As I completed each block, I marveled at how sharp the angles and points were and at how tiny I could make the patchwork. Paper piecing miniature patchwork presented new design opportunities and challenges. Just as the excitement of paper piecing had me hooked in my first three books, I knew that paper piecing miniatures was the beginning of another exciting adventure.

Several years ago, I wrote a magazine column entitled "Traveling Down a New Path." In this article, I wrote that if you approached your patchwork from a different perspective, you might discover new ideas. Looking back to consider which block designs from my previous books might work well in miniature, I began to look forward to what might be. And the blocks led naturally to designing miniature paper-pieced borders.

All it took was the completion of one miniature quilt, and I was already cutting the pieces for another. I was hooked once more, having fun and on my way to being a miniature-quilt enthusiast.

INTRODUCTION

The most common reaction from quilters who see miniature patchwork quilts for the first time is "Wow, I could never do that!" If that's your reaction, don't panic; this book will show you just how easy it is.

This book is a little different from my previous machine paper-piecing books. The previous books focus on blocks more than whole quilts. In this book, the focus is on complete miniature-quilt designs: paper-pieced blocks and accompanying borders.

The first section, "Miniature Quilts," defines a miniature quilt, then "Fabric" introduces you to the importance of print scale and fabric value (the lightness or darkness of a color).

"Block Designs" explains how to use the patterns and make paper foundations. This section also describes how to use the block-front drawings published in my previous books for miniature quilts. "Paper-Piecing Technique" explains the mechanics of machine paper piecing and includes tips on sewing miniature patchwork easily and efficiently.

Choose your favorite quilt from the color photos in the gallery, then go to "Projects" for step-by-step directions. "Finishing" leads you through the final steps. When you've made your way through the book, sit back and watch the expressions on the faces of your friends and family as they marvel at your miniature-quilt accomplishments.

MINIATURE QUILTS

Just because a quilt is small doesn't mean it's a miniature. The generally recognized size for miniature quilts is 24" square or less. But a miniature quilt should not only be small, it should also represent a scaled-down version of a full-size project (either a wall quilt or a bed quilt). For example, suppose your quilt is composed of six blocks across and six blocks down that are each 1" square. If each 1" block represents a scaled-down version of a 12" block, then your 6" x 6" quilt is one-twelfth of a 72"-square project. If the same 1" block represents a scaled-down version of a 10" block, then your quilt is one-tenth of a 60"-square project.

The following illustrations show two patchwork projects that are the same size. The first project is a small quilt, not a miniature quilt, because it doesn't represent a scaled-down version of a larger project. The second project is a good representation of a miniature because it could be made as a full-size quilt.

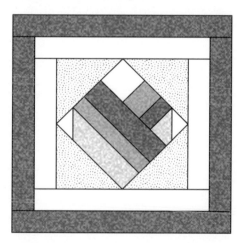

Small Quilt

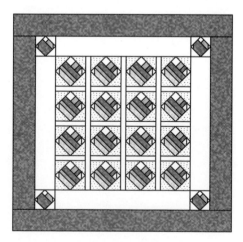

Miniature Quilt

FABRIC

Since a miniature quilt is a smaller version of a full-size project, the fabric should reflect that. Obvious first choices are solid fabrics because they have no design or texture that might look out of scale. However, don't discount small-scale prints. When considering printed fabrics, keep in mind the size of the patch or patches where the print will be used.

◆ A small-scale print may be too large for a tiny patch but just right for a bigger area.

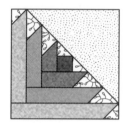

   This fabric does not work well in the small triangles in the first block, but it works fine in the large triangle in the second block.

◆ Tone-on-tone fabrics work well because they add subtle texture to the patchwork designs.

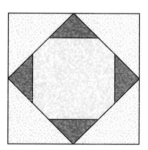

◆ A medium-scale print can take the place of a large-scale print used in a full-size project.

◆ Large-scale prints don't work well because the design gets lost when the fabric is cut into units.

 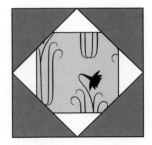

◆ TIP ◆

To see how a fabric will look in a block, audition it with a window template. Cut out the portion of the paper foundation where you intend to use the fabric. Place the window over the fabric to see if the fabric works. If it doesn't, try another fabric.

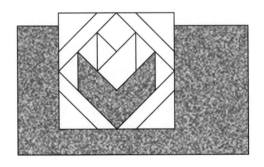

◆ ◆ ◆

USING DIRECTIONAL FABRICS

I usually avoid directional fabrics so I don't have to consider fabric grain or design orientation.

Directional fabric: Use a directional fabric when it will be placed only once in a block, or if it must be used more than once, only when it can be used in a consistent fashion. For example, the first illustration shows a check fabric used in just one location. The second illustration shows a check fabric used in a consistent fashion, along 45°-angle seams. The third illustration shows what happens when a check fabric is used at more than one angle: the check goes every which way.

 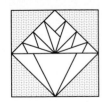 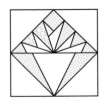

Small-scale stripe: Position the stripes so that you will sew across them rather than parallel to them. If the fabric moves as you stitch, it won't be as noticeable.

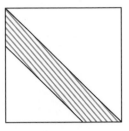 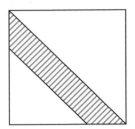

Do not try to sew in the same direction as stripes.   Sew against the direction of stripes.

WORKING WITH VALUE

Value is the lightness or darkness of a color; a black-and-white photograph shows only value. Contrasting values make a patchwork design stand out from the background.

◆ The smaller the patch, the greater the contrast required to make the design distinct. In the following example, the basket design is lost because small patches that make up the basket are too close in value to the background. In the second example, the basket stands out.

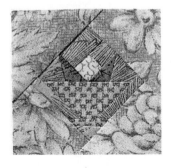 

◆ TIP ◆

If this is your first miniature experience, using high-contrast values may be a big adjustment. I suggest you make a trial block with your fabric choices before cutting all the pieces for a quilt.

◆ ◆ ◆

◆ Make sure tiny pieces contrast sharply with the patchwork around them—tiny pieces have less area in which to make an impact.

◆ Remember that you can use either side of your fabric. The change in value and texture may be just what you need.

◆ Consider low-contrast values when you don't want a patchwork detail to stand out. In the first example, low-contrast values blend to make the tree. In the second example, high-contrast values make each patch in the tree stand out.

LOOKING FOR FABRIC MOTIFS

Some prints contain wonderful motifs that can be centered in patchwork segments. Notice the floral motif in the basket in "Amish Baskets" (page 73). In "Country Baskets" (page 77), a floral motif is centered in the Geometric blocks. And in "Tree of Life Medallion" and "Christmas Bell Medallion" (page 79), a fabric motif in the Geometric blocks adds interest to the center of the quilt design as well as to the borders.

The best spot for a design motif is area #1 of the paper foundation. To audition fabric motifs, cut out area #1 from the foundation. Move the paper pattern around on the fabric to see what opportunities exist. See "Centering a Motif" on pages 11–12 for directions on cutting out fabric motifs.

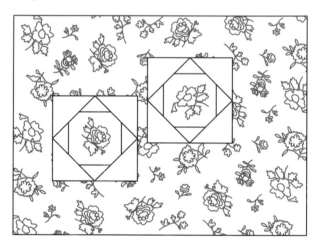

Audition design elements.

BLOCK DESIGNS

Full-size paper-piecing designs are provided on pages 96–111. The designs on these pages represent the wrong side of the completed patchwork. Smaller block-front drawings provided with the quilt directions show how the designs will appear from the fabric side when they are finished. The block-front drawings do not depict the actual size of the blocks and borders.

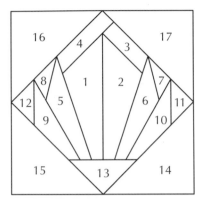

Paper-piecing design   Block-front drawing

If a design is symmetrical, the lined side of the foundation and the finished patchwork will look the same. In an asymmetrical design, the finished patchwork will be the reverse of the foundation's lined side.

Symmetrical Design

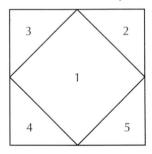
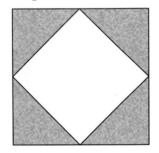

Lined side   Fabric side
Image is the same.

Asymmetrical Design

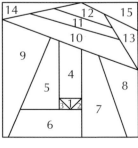
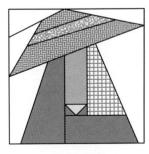

Lined side   Fabric side
Image is reversed.

USING PAPER FOUNDATIONS

In my previous paper-piecing books, you could reproduce the block designs by tracing them. I do not encourage that practice for these miniature designs. The intricate designs are not easy to trace accurately, and tracing paper will not withstand the smaller stitch length used for tiny blocks.

I recommend that you use a copy machine. Make all the copies for your quilt with the same copy machine from the original designs. Most copy machines slightly distort the original image—making a copy of a copy compounds the distortion. Use lightweight copy paper. It withstands the sewing process but is easy to remove.

For your convenience, preprinted foundations for all the quilts in this book are available from That Patchwork Place or your local quilt shop. Ask for Foundation Papers for Use with *Easy Paper-Pieced Miniatures*. Then you will have all the foundations you need to make a quilt—even if it's midnight.

Enlarging and Reducing

Use a copy machine to reduce or enlarge block designs. Reduce or enlarge border designs at the same percentage as the blocks in that quilt. For example, the 2" Fan blocks in "Jeweled Fans" (page 69) can be enlarged to 2½" by copying the 2" block design at 125%. You would also need to enlarge the corresponding 1¼" x 8" border by 125%, resulting in a border that is 1⁹⁄₁₆" x 10".

If math is not your thing, use a Proportional Scale to calculate percentages. Simply align the size of the original in the inner wheel with the desired size in the outer wheel; the percentage of enlargement or reduction appears in the window. Set the copy machine to the desired percentage to reproduce the new size.

◆ TIP ◆

Most copy shops can remove the binding of a book and either spiral-bind or three-hole punch the pages for a nominal fee. Then you can place the desired page flat on the bed of a copy machine.

◆ ◆ ◆

Cutting Out Foundations

I use my rotary cutter and rotary ruler to cut out copied foundations, ⅜" from the solid outer line. I then trim the block to ¼" from the outer line after completing the paper piecing. You can make several copies, staple them together, and rotary cut them all at once. Be sure to staple in an area where you will not be cutting.

USING BLOCK-FRONT DRAWINGS

More than two hundred block-front drawings can be found in my other paper-piecing books. They're just the right size for miniature quilts. They weren't designed to be used as piecing foundations, but you can use them that way once you're familiar with miniature paper-piecing techniques. The block-front drawings represent the finished side (or fabric side) of 4" block designs.

Easy Machine Paper Piecing: You'll find Geometric, Flower, Tree, Heart, Basket, and Picture blocks. The blocks in this book have few pieces.

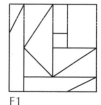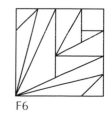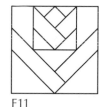

F1   F6   F11

Block-Front Drawings from *Easy Machine Paper Piecing*

Easy Paper-Pieced Keepsake Quilts: Designs include Geometric, Flower, Basket, Heart, Christmas, Picture, and Alphabet blocks. Some of the Alphabet blocks are asymmetrical. To use the block-front drawings for these, trace them onto a piece of tracing paper. Retrace the design on the reverse side and copy the reverse side to make the paper foundations.

A few of the blocks were created in sections, such as the Apple block shown below. While the full-size block designs are separated into sections, the block-front drawings are not. You must cut the block-front drawings to create the required paper-foundation sections. Cut ¼" beyond the joining seam for each section. You will need additional copies since you will destroy the foundation for the other section when you add the ¼"-wide seam allowance.

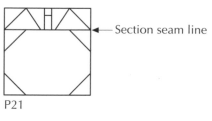

← Section seam line

P21

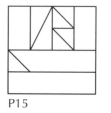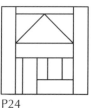

P15   P24

Block-Front Drawings from *Easy Paper-Pieced Keepsake Quilts*

Easy Mix & Match Machine Paper Piecing: One-inch designs include Geometric, Flower, and Picture blocks. Some of the block designs are sectioned; you can mix and match sections for even more design options.

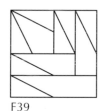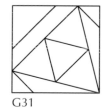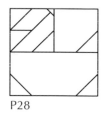

G31   F39   P28

Block-Front Drawings from
Easy Mix & Match Machine Paper Piecing

Easy Reversible Vests: Designs include Geometric, Flower, Heart, Basket, Tree, and Picture blocks. The full-size paper-piecing designs are 3" square and the block-front drawings are 1⅜" square. There are a few two-section blocks in this book.

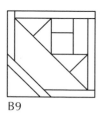

G19   F26   B9

Block-Front Drawings from *Easy Reversible Vests*

Since the blocks from the previous books were originally designed as 3" and 4" blocks, some of the block-front drawings may be too intricate for miniatures. To make the block-front drawings more useable, consider eliminating seams to simplify them. The following illustrations show how to simplify a block-front drawing.

1" x 1"

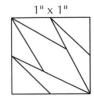

1" x 1"

G34 from *Easy Mix & Match Machine Paper Piecing*

Some seam lines eliminated.

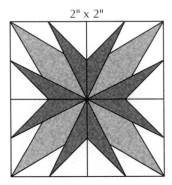

2" x 2"

Look what happens when you put four blocks together!

Sometimes, adding seams can make paper piecing even easier! For example, adding a seam line across a corner of a block can reduce the seams in the center of a four-block unit. The rule of thumb is, if you can continue the piecing sequence without encountering a subsequent intersecting seam, then you can add that seam line.

Seam line added

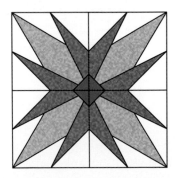

◆ TIP ◆

If the block-front drawings seem a bit small, reduce the full-size paper-piecing designs. Reducing a 3" block design by 50% will yield a 1½" block; reducing a 4" block design by 50% will yield a 2" block. Try different reductions until you get a size you can work with.

◆ ◆ ◆

PAPER-PIECING TECHNIQUES

GATHERING SUPPLIES

You'll find the following supplies helpful for miniature paper piecing.

- ◆ Sewing machine in good working order
- ◆ Size 90/14 sewing machine needle
- ◆ Standard sewing-weight thread that matches the values in your project
- ◆ Rotary cutter and rotary-cutting mat
- ◆ Thread clippers, which are easier on your hands than scissors for repeated snipping
- ◆ Rotary rulers—6" x 6" (with ⅛" lines) and 6" x 12"
- ◆ Add-An-Eighth Ruler, to make trimming patchwork pieces a breeze
- ◆ Self-adhesive sandpaper tabs. Attach these to the corners of your rotary rulers to keep them from slipping on fabric or paper.
- ◆ Straight silk pins with small heads
- ◆ Travel iron and pressing board set up next to your sewing machine. Cover your pressing board with a scrap of muslin to protect it from any ink that may transfer from photocopies.
- ◆ Small clip-on light next to the sewing machine to aid in placing fabric
- ◆ Removable Scotch Brand/Magic tape to repair the paper foundation if it should tear. Do not touch the tape with a hot iron.
- ◆ Pads of small stick-on notes for labeling fabric with piece numbers and block locations
- ◆ Tweezers for removing tiny bits of paper
- ◆ Stapler for attaching several copies of paper foundations together so they won't move as you cut them out
- ◆ A staple remover to save your fingernails

Cutting Fabric Pieces

Cutting fabric for miniature paper-pieced blocks is actually easier than cutting fabric for larger paper-pieced blocks.

◆ The grain of the fabric is not important, because the pieces are so small.

◆ Almost all the pieces are cut as squares, rectangles, and strips. In some cases, it is more efficient to cut triangles. See "Exceptions to the Rule" on page 13.

◆ One shape can often be used for a variety of different-size patches, because the variation in size is so slight.

A cutting chart is provided for each quilt project. Cut the binding, borders, and setting pieces across the width of the fabric first, then cut the pieces for the paper-pieced borders and blocks. When you see the symbol in the cutting chart, cut the square(s) once diagonally to make two half-square triangles.

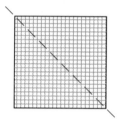

Half-Square Triangles

When you see the symbol in the cutting chart, cut the square(s) twice diagonally to make four quarter-square triangles.

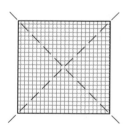

Quarter-Square Triangles

Cut several pieces at a time by layering fabric. For example, if you need 40 rectangles, each 1" x 2", cut a 2"-wide strip from folded fabric. Fold the strip in quarters and cut 1" segments from the layers. If you need the same size and shape from several different fabrics, layer the fabrics, then cut the required pieces all at once.

◆ TIP ◆

To keep your place, put a ruler or piece of paper under each line in the cutting chart. Attach small stick-on notes to each group of cut fabrics to indicate the placement number and block number. When you sew the blocks, you simply need to look at the notes to locate the next fabric piece in the sequence.

◆ ◆ ◆

Centering a Motif

To center a motif in area #1 of a foundation, follow these steps.

1. Cut out an extra paper foundation, ¼" from the solid outer line. Cut out area #1, where the fabric motif will be centered.

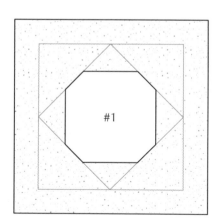

2. Attach the paper foundation to the corner of a rotary ruler with tape or a washable gluestick.

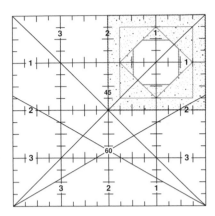

Attach foundation to the ruler.

3. Center the fabric motif in the cut-out area and cut on 2 adjacent sides of the ruler. Turn the fabric and align the just-cut fabric edges with the edge of the paper foundation. Cut the remaining 2 sides. Your motif is now centered in a piece of fabric that includes ample seam allowances.

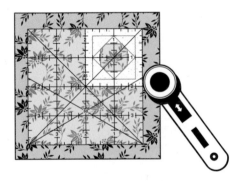

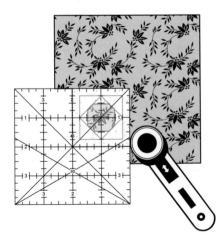

DETERMINING FABRIC-PIECE SIZE

Although cut sizes for fabric pieces are provided for the projects, it's helpful to know how to determine the cut size yourself. Even though you will trim seam allowances of patches inside the block to ⅛" and to ¼" along the outer edge, work with the premise that a minimum of ½" total for seam allowances is needed. Your fabric pieces will be larger than necessary.

Determine the smallest piece of fabric you can comfortably handle. For me, this was ¾" x 1". Therefore, I never cut anything smaller. Cut squares or rectangles unless otherwise noted.

If you're using one fabric in several patches that are slightly different in size, cut one size that will accommodate all the patches. The difference in size is not great enough to warrant cutting a variety of slightly different pieces. For example, if I need 20 squares that are 1½" and 30 squares that are 1¾", all from the same fabric, I would cut fifty 1¾" squares to use for both. I would not cut pieces of the same size if I needed sixty 1" squares and four 2" squares from the same fabric. I would cut sixty 1" squares and four 2" squares.

To determine the size to cut, place a rotary ruler over area #1 of the foundation. Cut a piece of fabric that will cover this area plus a generous ¼"-wide seam allowance on all sides. When piece #1 is an on-point square, you can place the ruler on point to take the measurement.

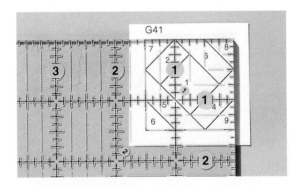

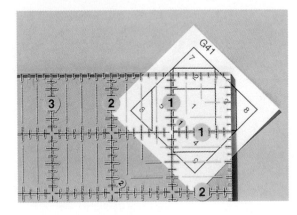

To cut fabric for the subsequent pieces in the block, place the ruler's ¼" mark on the seam line you will sew when you add that piece. Let the majority of the ruler fall over the patch. Look through the ruler to determine what size square or strip is needed to cover the area, and allow a generous ¼" seam allowance on all sides.

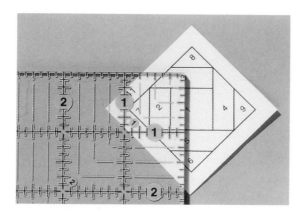

Exceptions to the Rule

It's sometimes faster and more efficient to cut half-square and quarter-square triangles for the required pieces, since fabric grain doesn't matter within the patchwork block. When a block requires half-square triangles along the outer edge, cut squares and then cut them once diagonally. To determine what size to cut the square, measure the short side of the triangle and add 1¼" to this measurement.

Cutting Half-Square Triangles

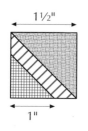
1½"
1"

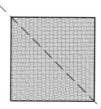
1½" + 1¼" = 2¾"

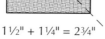

1" + 1¼" = 2¼"

◆ **TIP** ◆

If you are using a directional print for half-square triangles that will be placed on the outer edges of a block, cut two squares, then cut them once diagonally in opposite directions to continue the design through the block. If you want to cut several triangles, layer 2 strips of fabric—either right sides together or wrong sides together—cut squares, and then cut the squares once diagonally. The directional print in the second layer of triangles will be a mirror image of the first layer.

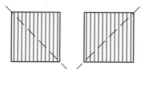

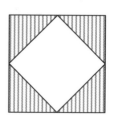

Wrong side

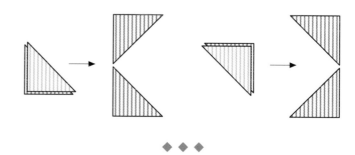

◆ ◆ ◆

If you need multiple triangles, cutting quarter-square triangles from one square is quick. To determine what size to cut the square, measure the long side of the triangle and add 1½" to this measurement.

Cutting Quarter-Square Triangles

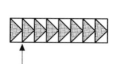
The length of the long side of the triangle is ¾".

¾" + 1½" = 2¼"

PREPARING TO PAPER PIECE

To set the stage for miniature paper piecing, insert a size 90/14 needle in your sewing machine and set the stitch length at 20 to 23 stitches per inch. If your machine's stitch length ranges from 0 to 5, set it just above 1. Before you begin, test your stitches on copy paper with fabric underneath, and adjust the stitch length as needed. You don't want to tear the paper as you sew, but you do want the stitch to be as small as possible and still keep the paper intact.

Use a regular sewing-weight thread in a color that blends with the majority of your fabrics. Off-white thread for light quilts, medium gray for quilts with a variety of values, and black for dark quilts is fine.

It's easiest to stitch on the line when you can see it clearly, so use a presser foot with an open toe (sometimes called an open-toe embroidery foot).

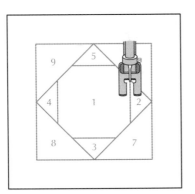

Set up a rotary-cutting area on one side of the sewing machine and a pressing area on the other. Cover your pressing board with a scrap of muslin to absorb any copy-machine ink that might transfer while you press. I use a small travel iron on a cotton setting with no steam.

Use a small lamp or clip-on light next to the sewing machine so you will be able to see through the paper easily when positioning the first piece of fabric.

SEWING TECHNIQUES

STEP-BY-STEP SEWING

For the purpose of illustration, a tracing-paper foundation and contrasting thread are shown.
The T16 block was enlarged to 2" to make it easier to see.

1. Select the appropriate paper foundations for the quilt you are making.

2. Cut out the paper foundation ⅜" from the outer solid line. Consider the lined side of the foundation as the "mechanical side." From this side, you'll do only mechanical things, such as measure for fabric pieces and sew. Consider the blank side of the foundation as the "visual side." To place fabrics, you'll look through the blank side to the design on the other side. This way, what you see is what you get and you don't need to think in reverse.

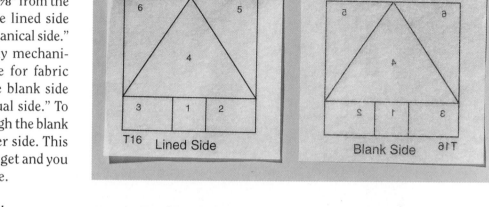

3. Using a light source to help you see through the foundation, place the fabric for piece #1, right side up, on the blank side of the paper, over the area marked #1. Make sure the fabric covers the area and extends at least ¼" beyond all seam lines. Pin the fabric in place with a small-head pin. Place the pin away from the seam line between pieces #1 and #2.

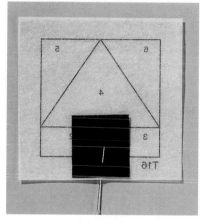
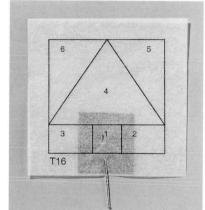

4. Place a 3" x 5" index card or a postcard (glossy side up) on the line between #1 and #2. Fold the paper along the edge of the postcard to expose the excess fabric beyond the first seam line.

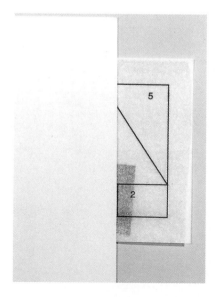
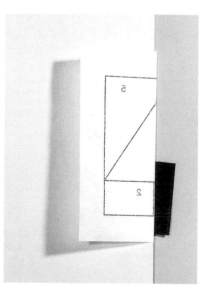

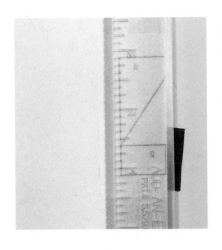
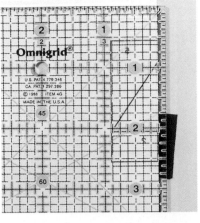

5. Place an Add-An-Eighth ruler on the fold (or use the ⅛" line on a rotary ruler) and trim the excess fabric ⅛" from the fold. This method of folding the fabric along the next seam to be sewn is known as the "card trick." It not only allows you to trim the previous fabrics to ⅛", permitting easy alignment of the subsequent fabric(s), but it also weakens the paper so it is easier to remove.

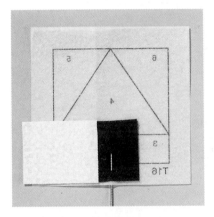
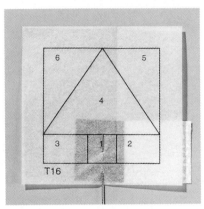

6. Place piece #2 right side up over the area it needs to cover, looking through the blank side of the paper to confirm correct placement.

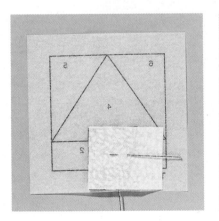
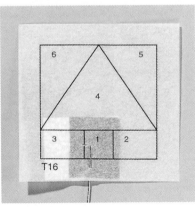

7. Place piece #2 right sides together with piece #1 and pin in place. The cotton fabrics should cling to each other; however, pinning will help if you're just learning to paper piece. As you become comfortable with paper piecing, you probably won't need to pin subsequent pieces. If you use slippery fabrics, you'll want to pin.

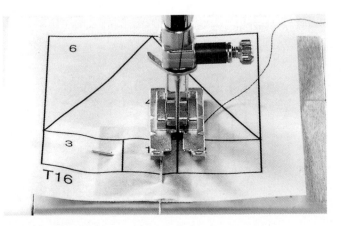

8. Carefully place the paper foundation and pinned fabrics under your presser foot. Sew on the line between spaces #1 and #2. Begin sewing about ¼" before the line and extend the stitching about ¼" beyond the end.

9. Cut the threads, open piece #2, and press.

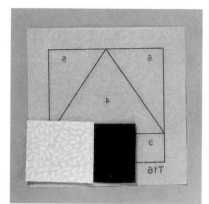 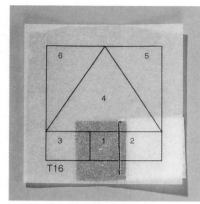

10. Continue with piece #3 by placing the card on the line between #1 and #3. Fold the paper back along the line between #1 and #3, then trim the excess fabrics ⅛" beyond the fold.

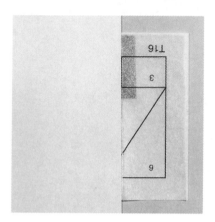 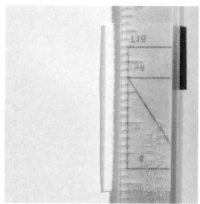

11. To determine correct placement, place piece #3 right side up over the area it needs to cover, then place it right sides together with piece #1. Pin in place and sew on the line between #1 and #3. Clip the threads, open piece #3, and press.

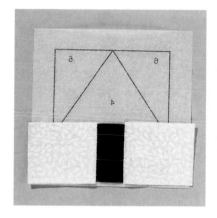 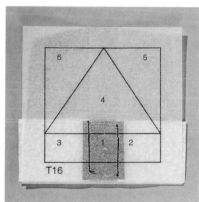

12. Continue the procedure with piece #4. This time, when you fold the paper back along the line that joins #4 with the previous pieces, you'll notice some previous stitching. Just pull the paper away so it will fold along line #4.

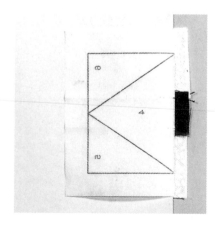

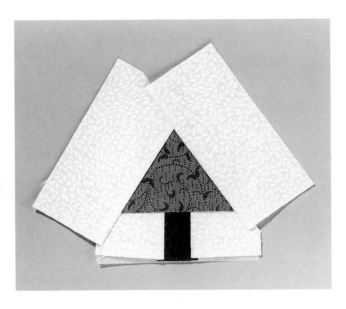

13. Continue adding fabrics in numerical order.

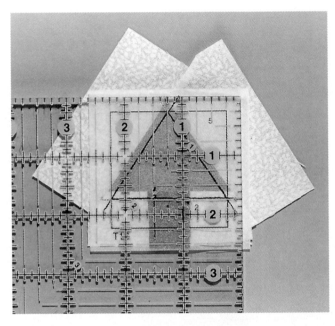

14. Trim the block ¼" from the outer line. Align the ¼" markings on the ruler on the solid lines at both the top and side of the block to trim both edges without moving the ruler. Turn the block around to trim the remaining 2 sides in the same manner. Do not remove the paper!

Note: I experimented with ⅛"-wide seam allowances around the outer edge of the paper foundations but had better control with ¼"-wide seam allowances and didn't find the seams too bulky. You can trim the outer seam allowances to ⅛" after you sew the seams if you prefer.

PAPER-PIECING TIPS

◆ When adding triangle pieces, look through the blank side of the foundation to the design on the other side. Place the fabric right side up on the blank side, over the area it will cover, to confirm correct placement.

◆ When placing triangle pieces right sides together with previously stitched piece(s), align the corner of the fabric triangle with the corner of the triangle on the foundation. This will assure that the triangle is centered over the area.

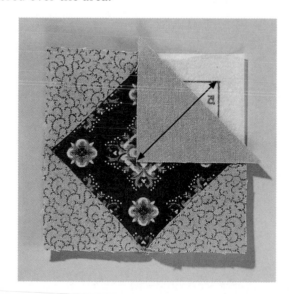

◆ When centering a fabric motif in area #1, use a light source to aid in placement and pin the fabric securely in place.

◆ If the paper should tear while you are working, repair it with removable tape. Do not touch the iron directly to the tape. Do not use cellophane tape—it will melt even if it is not touched directly by the iron.

◆ When trimming the blocks, use a ruler with ¼" lines on two sides.

◆ Use a small stitch length when sewing tiny areas and a bit larger stitch length when sewing long pieces, such as border strips.

◆ Attach the Add-An-Eighth ruler to the 3" x 5" card or postcard so you pick up one item rather than two. If you are right-handed, place the ⅛" lip of the ruler along the right edge of the card. Layer two 3" pieces of ¾" masking tape and tape the top of the ruler to the card to make a hinge. If you are left-handed, attach the ruler as described to the left side of the card. Attaching the ruler to the card won't work with long paper-pieced borders.

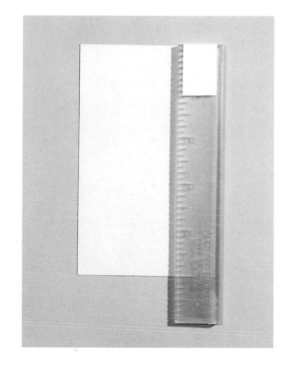

Sewing and Pressing

You are less likely to make a mistake if you develop a routine for cutting and stitching— and your project will move along faster. For example, if you cut pieces from folded fabric, place all the pieces in a neat stack with the same side up. If you leave them in the stack facing both right and wrong side up, you'll have to manipulate the fabric pieces before placing them on the foundation.

Fast Feeding

Feed the fabrics and foundations assembly-line fashion. Don't bother to cut the thread between the foundations, but gently pull the just-sewn foundation toward the back until the presser-foot area is clear to feed the next foundation. On your work table, orient all the foundation blocks in the same direction so you don't have to manipulate the foundation direction.

Fast Pressing and Trimming

Place the entire string of blocks, paper side up, on the ironing board. Clip the threads between the blocks on the paper side, close to the paper. Pick up one end and flip the string of blocks to the fabric side. Clip the remaining threads on the fabric side, close to the fabric. Press the just-joined fabric pieces open with a dry iron on the cotton setting.

Stack the blocks uniformly, paper side up, so the just-sewn pieces are ready to be trimmed ⅛" from the next sewing line. Trim the pieces assembly-line style, again orienting the trimmed blocks in the same way on your work table. You are now ready to pick up the next stack of fabrics and add the next piece.

Joining Block Sections, Rows, and Borders

When it is time to join block sections, rows, and borders, I strongly recommend that you machine baste the beginning and end of each seam and any matching points before you sew. Because you are using such a small stitch length, even if the units align properly when you begin, they will probably be off when you finish the seam. Machine basting not only gives you a second chance for a perfect match, but it forces any easing to occur in areas where it won't matter. It's not necessary to clip the thread between the basting areas; simply pull the block to the next basting area. I know this may seem like extra effort, and it may be tempting to skip this step, but it will make the difference between everything going along as it should and frustration.

To join paper-pieced blocks, rows, or borders:
1. Trim the block or section ¼" from the outer line.
2. Place the units to be joined right sides together. Pin the pieces, placing the pins away from the sewing line.

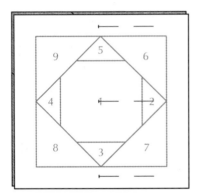

3. Machine baste the beginning, any matching points, and the end. Remove the pins and open the unit to check for a good match.

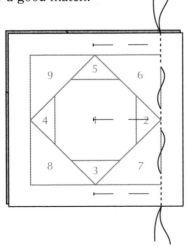

◆ TIP ◆

Before you baste, insert the sewing machine needle in the middle of the seam line of the piece on top. Remove the pieces to see if the needle is in the seam line of the bottom unit. If it isn't, your blocks may not be aligned properly, or the seam allowance on the edge of the block(s) may not be exactly ¼" wide. This "needle check" is simple to do, and if something is wrong, you'll know before you begin basting.

◆ ◆ ◆

4. If, after basting, everything is as it should be, sew the seam with a small stitch. If you need to fix an area, simply remove the basting stitches by cutting the thread from the bobbin side and pulling the thread. Realign, pin, and baste again.

When joining a row of blocks made from two sections, press the joining seam allowances in opposite directions.

Press seam allowances from the fabric side in opposite directions from row to row, unless otherwise indicated. This will lock the seam intersections when you join the rows. In the quiltmaking illustrations, arrows indicate which way to press seam allowances.

Border Tips

◆ For border units, when #1 and #2 are long fabric strips, pin them, right sides together, ⅛" from the first seam line without doing the card trick.

◆ When adding paper-pieced borders to strips of fabric, pin the units well and baste with the paper-pieced border still on top. When everything is accurate, sew with the paper-pieced border on top.

◆ When sewing two fabric strips together—without a paper foundation—use a normal stitch length (twelve stitches per inch). Change back to the smaller stitch length when sewing across a paper foundation.

◆ When sewing on paper-pieced foundations, you will follow the stitching line. However, when sewing through the cut fabric pieces, there is no line; be sure to sew with a ¼" seam allowance.

REMOVING THE PAPER

Don't remove the paper until the miniature quilt top is complete. To remove the paper, gently tug against the stitching lines until the paper pulls away from the stitching. Try not to tear the paper into small pieces—it takes more time to remove more pieces. For really tiny pieces, use tweezers. This is one of those activities you can do while watching TV, talking on the phone, or listening to your favorite music.

PROJECTS

My goal was to create miniature quilts that appear difficult to make, but in reality are not. All measurements listed in the Paper-Piecing Information at a Glance boxes are finished sizes. The finished size of the quilt does not include the ¼" seam allowances on the outer edge of the last border or the binding area. The cut sizes for borders are shown in the quilt plans.

The block-front drawings represent the finished (fabric) side of the blocks and borders. I numbered these block designs consecutively by categories, continuing from my other paper-piecing books. For example, the Basket block in "Mini Amish Baskets" is number B13 because my last Basket block design was B12, published in *Easy Paper-Pieced Keepsake Quilts*. The following categories are included in this book:

> G—Geometric Blocks
> F—Flower Blocks
> B—Basket Blocks
> H—Heart Blocks
> T—Tree Blocks
> P—Picture Blocks
> PB—Pieced Borders

Fabric requirements are provided for each quilt; I used a ⅛-yard minimum when a fabric is used several times. When I was able to just squeak out the fabric pieces from a prewashed piece of fabric, I increased the yardage to the next increment so you would be sure to have enough.

Follow the cutting charts carefully. To simplify the cutting, a cut size is often given that will accommodate several different-size patches. When the pieces are this small, using a bit of extra fabric doesn't amount to much. Cut squares once diagonally when you see the ◹ symbol and twice diagonally when you see the ⊠ symbol.

The one-sided arrows in the illustrations indicate the pressing direction for the seam allowances. Follow these arrows as you assemble your patchwork. When joining blocks in rows, press the seam allowances in opposite directions from row to row.

The block foundations are arranged on one page for each quilt, so you can easily photocopy them. Extra patterns for practice or auditioning fabric selections are included. Some patterns do not include a dotted cutting line on all sides of the patterns. In these cases, cut ⅜" from the solid outside line of the pattern.

Reminders

◆ Make a trial block to audition fabric choices before you cut all the pieces for the quilt. See "Fabric" on pages 5–7.
◆ Attach a stick-on note to each group of cut pieces to indicate the patch number(s) and block or border location in which they will be used. See page 11.
◆ Place a piece of paper or a ruler under each line in the cutting chart to help you keep on track.
◆ Follow the pressing arrows.
◆ Have fun!

Amish Baskets

For this quilt, I wanted to feature a small-scale floral motif inside the basket handles. Choose your floral fabric first and audition the motif in the rectangular space. Cut this space out of an extra paper pattern and move the pattern around the fabric to see how the flowers will look in the space. See page 7.

For the background of the Basket block, choose a solid fabric or mini-print that matches the background color of the floral print. For the basket, select a fabric that contrasts in color and value with the floral print so the basket stands out.

Although at first glance the blocks appear to be set diagonally, they are actually set in a straight grid. The corner triangles in the Basket blocks look as though they are alternate blocks in the finished quilt. To camouflage the seams, choose a non-directional print for the corner triangles .

Materials

¼ yd. black for blocks, outer border, and binding
⅛ yd. black floral
¼ yd. blue for blocks and inner border
¼ yd. gray
13" x 13" square of fabric for backing
13" x 13" square of batting

Black   Black floral   Blue   Gray

Finished Quilt Size: 11" x 11"
Color photo on page 73.

PAPER-PIECING INFORMATION AT A GLANCE			
Paper-Pieced Units	Block/ Border No.	No. to Make	Finished Size of Unit
Basket Block	B13	9	2½" x 2½"
Pieced Border	PB1	4	1¾" x 7½"
Corner Blocks	G39	4	1¾" x 1¾"

B13   G39   PB1

Block-Front Drawings
Full-size patterns are on page 96.

CUTTING FOR BINDING		
Fabric	No. of Pieces	Dimensions
Black	1	1¾" x 40"
	1	1¾" x 20"

CUTTING FOR BLOCKS AND PAPER-PIECED BORDERS				
Fabric	No. of Pieces	Dimensions	Patch No.	Block/Border No.
Black	4	2" x 8½"	1	PB1
	4	2½" x 2½"	1	G39
	18	2" x 2" ◺	5–7	B13 top
			5	B13 bottom
	18	¾" x 2¼"	2, 3	B13 bottom
Black floral	9	1½" x 1½"	1	B13 top*
Blue	4	1½" x 8½"	2	PB1
	2	2" x 2" ◺	2	G39
	9	2½" x 1½"	1	B13 bottom
	36	¾" x 1½"	2–4	B13 top
			4	B13 bottom
Gray	18	2½" x 2½" ◺	8, 9	B13 top
			6, 7	B13 bottom

*Center a fabric motif in each square. See pages 11–12.

Directions

1. Make 5 copies of page 96. Cut out patterns on the dotted lines for:
   9 Basket blocks (B13, both top and bottom)
   4 Geometric corner blocks (G39)
   4 pieced borders (PB1)
2. Make the blocks, placing fabrics as shown.

3. Make the pieced borders, placing fabrics as shown.

PB1
Make 4.

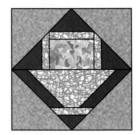

B13
Make 9.

G39
Make 4.

4. Sew the Basket blocks (B13) into horizontal rows. Join the rows.

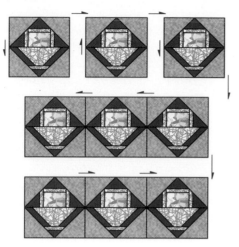

5. Sew pieced borders to the sides of the quilt top. Add a corner block (G39) to each end of the remaining borders as shown, then sew them to the top and bottom edges of the quilt top.

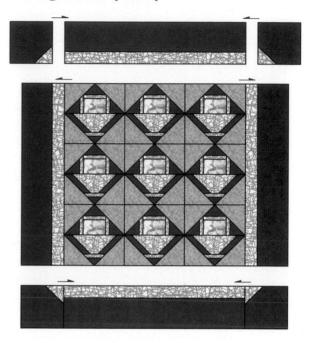

6. Referring to "Finishing" on pages 90–94, layer your quilt top with batting and backing; baste. Quilt as desired and bind the edges.

Little Nosegays

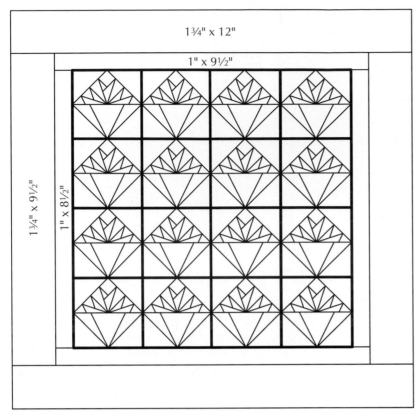

1¾" x 12"

1" x 9½"

1¾" x 9½"

1" x 8½"

Finished Quilt Size: 11½" x 11½"
Measurements in quilt plan are cut sizes.
Color photo on page 68.

PAPER-PIECING INFORMATION AT A GLANCE			
Paper-Pieced Unit	Block/ Border No.	No. to Make	Finished Size of Unit
Flower Blocks	F72	16	2" x 2"

F72

Block-Front Drawing
Full-size pattern is on page 97.

Several years ago, an antique Nosegay quilt featuring a variety of pastel scraps caught my attention. "Little Nosegays" was inspired by that memory. This quilt is a great opportunity to use up solid-color scraps. The first time I made this quilt, I used a light background and pastel solids. Then I made it using a black background and jewel tones. The different color scheme produced a dramatically different look. A central focus is achieved by simply changing the fabric in the outer triangles of the block.

Simplify the cutting by layering several solid-color scrap fabrics so you can cut multiple pieces at once.

Materials

¼ yd. black floral for blocks, outer border, and binding
⅛ yd. fuchsia for inner border
¼ yd. black
⅛ yd. teal
⅛ yd. total assorted solids
⅛ yd. purple
13" x 13" square of fabric for backing
13" x 13" square of batting

Black floral

Fuchsia

Black

Teal

Assorted solids

Purple

CUTTING BORDERS AND BINDING			
Fabric	No. of Pieces	Dimensions	Location
Black floral	2	1¾" x 12"	Top and bottom outer borders
	2	1¾" x 9½"	Side outer borders
	1	1¾" x 40"	Binding
	1	1¾" x 20"	Binding
Fuchsia	2	1" x 9½"	Top and bottom inner borders
	2	1" x 8½"	Side inner borders

CUTTING FOR BLOCKS				
Fabric	No. of Pieces	Dimensions	Patch No.	Block No.
Black	112	1" x 1½"	1, 4, 5, 8, 9, 12, 13	F72 top
	32	1" x 2"	2, 3	F72 bottom
Teal	16	1½" x 1¾"	1	F72 bottom
Assorted solids	96	1" x 1¼"	2, 3, 6, 7, 10, 11	F72 top
Black floral	14	2¼" x 2¼" ◩	14, 15	F72 top*
			4, 5	F72 bottom*
Purple	18	2¼" x 2¼" ◩	14, 15	F72 top*
			4, 5	F72 bottom*

See step 2 for placement.

Directions

1. Make 4 copies of page 97. Cut out patterns on the dotted lines for:
    16 Flower blocks (F72)
2. Make the blocks, placing fabrics as shown. Since the fabric placement for the top sections is identical through #13, and the bottom sections identical through #3, make these sections in assembly-line fashion.

F72
Make 1.

F72
Make 2.

F72
Make 1.

F72
Make 1.

F72
Make 2.

F72
Make 4.

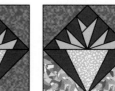

F72
Make 2.

F72
Make 2.

F72
Make 1.

3. Sew the blocks into horizontal rows. Join the rows.

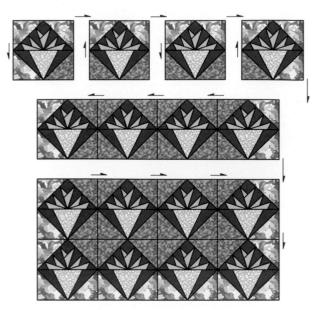

4. Sew the 1" x 8½" fuchsia strips to the sides of the quilt top. Sew the remaining fuchsia strips to the top and bottom edges. Repeat with the 1¾"-wide black floral strips for the outer borders.

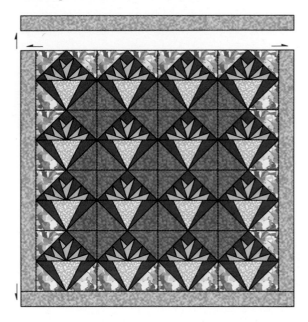

5. Referring to "Finishing" on pages 90–94, layer your quilt top with batting and backing; baste. Quilt as desired and bind the edges.

Mariner's Compass

1¼" x 1¼"　　　　　　　　　　　　　　　1⅝" x 1⅝"

1¼" x 9"

1⅝" x 6¾"

Finished Quilt Size: 10" x 10"
Measurements in quilt plan are cut sizes.
Color photo on page 66.

*T*his interpretation of Mariner's Compass is easy to do because paper foundations make intricate piecing a breeze. Four Geometric blocks combine to create the compass. To continue the nautical theme, I used various shades of blue, with a few purples to add excitement. The blue and purple fabrics I used in the borders and corner squares also appear in the flying-geese borders, along with a variety of other scraps.

Materials

¼ yd. dark blue for outer border and binding
⅛ yd. purple for corner squares
⅛ yd. light blue for inner border
¼ yd. white
⅛ yd. total assorted blues and purples
12" x 12" square of fabric for backing
12" x 12" square of batting

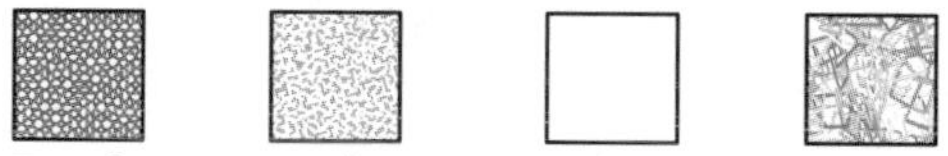

Purple　　Light blue　　White　　Assorted blues and purples

PAPER-PIECING INFORMATION AT A GLANCE			
Paper-Pieced Units	Block/ Border No.	No. to Make	Finished Size of Unit
Geometric blocks	G40	4	1½" x 1½"*
Pieced borders	PB2	2	1⅝" x 3"
	PB3	2	1⅝" x 6¼"

Makes 3" Mariner's Compass

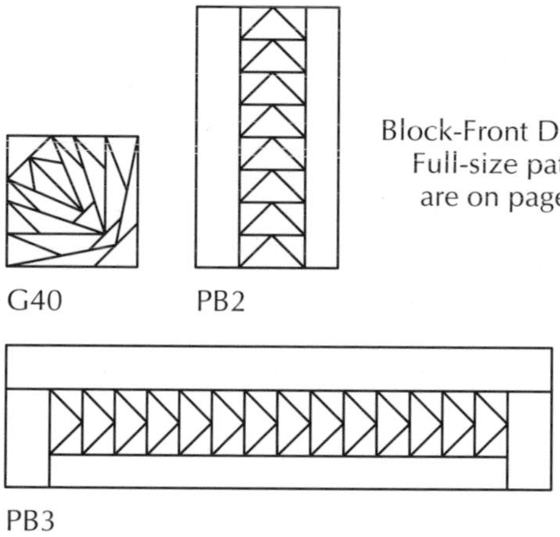

G40　　　PB2

Block-Front Drawings
Full-size patterns
are on page 99.

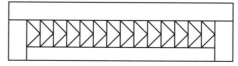

PB3

CUTTING CORNER SQUARES, BORDERS, AND BINDING			
Fabric	No. of Pieces	Dimensions	Location
Dark blue	4	1¼" x 9"	Outer border
	1	1¾" x 40"	Binding
	1	1¾" x 6"	Binding
Purple	4	1⅝" x 1⅝"	Inner corner squares
	4	1¼" x 1¼"	Outer corner squares
Light blue	4	1⅝" x 6¾"	Inner border

Fabric	No. of Pieces	Dimensions	Location Number	Block/Border
White	2	1¼" x 7½"	46	PB3
	2	1¼" x 6¼"	26	PB2*
			44, 45	PB3*
	2	1¼" x 4"	25	PB2
	2	1¼" x 6"	43	PB3
	36	1½" x 1"	3–5, 9, 10, 13, 14, 18, 19	G40
	44	1¾" x 1¾" ◻	**	PB2, PB3
Asst. blues & purples	52	1" x 2"	1, 2, 6–8, 11, 12, 15–17, 20–22	G40
	11	2¼" x 2¼" ⊠	***	PB2, PB3

Add side borders after PB2 and PB3 have been joined to the center compass. See step 8.

**Use for small triangles in flying geese borders.*

***Use for large triangles in flying geese borders.*

Directions

1. Make 2 copies of page 99. Cut out patterns on the dotted lines for:
   - 4 Geometric blocks (G40)
   - 2 pieced borders for sides (PB2)
   - 2 pieced borders for top and bottom (PB3)
2. Make 4 Geometric blocks (G40), using assorted blues and purples, and white. I used the same fabrics to make 4 identical blocks.

G40
Make 4.

3. Join the Geometric blocks (G40) to create the Mariner's Compass. When joining the two halves, remove the paper in the seam allowance to reduce bulk.

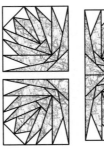 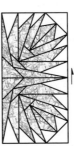 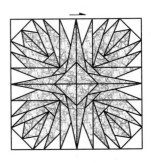

4. Make 2 side borders (PB2) through piece #25, using assorted blues and purples, and white. Fold the paper back along line #26 and trim the excess fabric ⅛" from the fold, but do not add piece #26 yet.

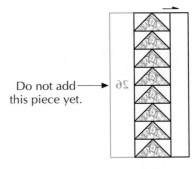

Do not add → this piece yet.

Make 2.

5. Sew a side border (PB2) to each side of the unit made in step 3.

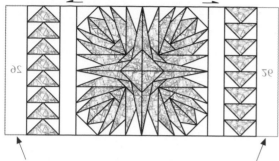

The fabric pieces have not yet been added for #26.

6. Make the top and bottom borders (PB3) through piece #43, using assorted blues and purples, and white. Fold the paper back along lines #44, #45, and #46, then trim excess fabric ⅛" from the folds, but do not add pieces #44, #45, and #46 yet.

The fabric has not yet been added in these places.

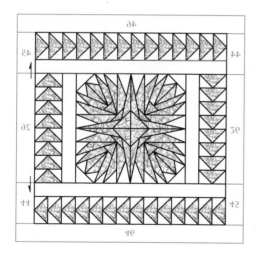

Make 2.

7. Sew the top and bottom borders to the quilt top.

8. Sew 1¼" x 6¼" white strips across pieces #26, #44, and #45. Add piece #46 to the top and bottom edges.

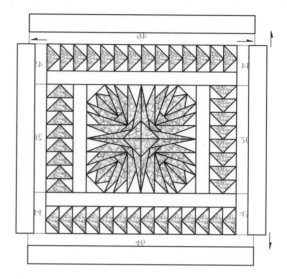

9. Sew light blue inner border strips to the sides of the quilt top. Add a large purple square to each end of the remaining light blue inner border strips, then sew the strips to the top and bottom edges.

10. Add the dark blue outer border and the small purple corner squares in the same fashion.

11. Referring to "Finishing" on pages 90–94, layer your quilt top with batting and backing; baste. Quilt as desired and bind the edges.

Flower Trellis

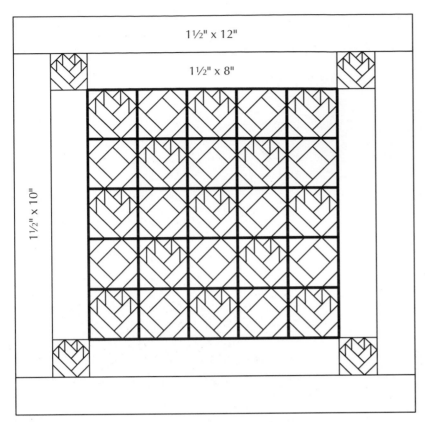

1½" x 12"

1½" x 8"

1½" x 10"

Finished Quilt Size: 11½" x 11½"
Measurements in quilt plan are cut sizes.
Color photo on page 72.

This quilt combines a Flower block with a simple geometric design. Careful fabric placement accentuates the trellis to make an intricate looking quilt. To make the tiny pieces stand out, make sure adjacent pieces contrast strongly in value.

Materials

⅓ yd. black for blocks and outer border
¼ yd. black floral for blocks, inner border, and binding
⅛ yd. white
⅛ yd. light pink
⅛ yd. medium pink
⅛ yd. medium-dark pink
⅛ yd. dark pink
⅛ yd. light green
⅛ yd. medium green
⅛ yd. dark green
13" x 13" square of fabric for backing
13" x 13" square of batting

Black	Black floral	White	Light pink

Medium pink	Medium-dark pink	Dark pink

Light green	Medium green	Dark green

PAPER-PIECING INFORMATION AT A GLANCE

Paper-Pieced Units	Block/ Border No.	No. to Make	Finished Size of Unit
Large Flower block	F73	13	1½" x 1½"
Small Flower block	F73	4	1" x 1"
Geometric block	G41	12	1½" x 1½"

F73   G41

Block-Front Drawings
Full-size patterns are on page 98.

CUTTING BORDERS AND BINDING

Fabric	No. of Pieces	Dimensions	Location
Black	2	1½" x 10"	Side outer borders
	2	1½" x 12"	Top & bottom outer borders
Black floral	1	1¾" x 40"	Binding
	1	1¾" x 14"	Binding
	4	1½" x 8"	Inner border

CUTTING FOR BLOCKS

Fabric	No. of Pieces	Dimensions	Location Number	Block
White	85	1" x 1¼"	1, 3, 5, 8, 9	F73 both sizes
	12	1" x 2"	3	G41
Light pink	17	1" x 1¼"	4	F73 both sizes
Medium pink	17	1" x 1"	2	F73 both sizes
Medium-dark pink	17	1" x 1¼"	6	F73 both sizes
Dark pink	17	1" x 1¾"	7	F73 both sizes
Light green	12	1" x 2¼"	5	G41
Medium green	29	1" x 2¼"	4	G41
			11	F73 both sizes
Dark green	29	1" x 2"	2	G41
			10	F73 both sizes
Black	58	1¾" x 1¾" ◻	12–15	F73 both sizes
			6–9	G41
Black floral	12	1½" x 1½"	1	G41

Directions

1. Make 3 copies of page 98. Cut out patterns on the dotted lines for:
   - 12 Geometric blocks (G41)
   - 13 large Flower blocks (F73)
   - 4 small Flower blocks (F73)
2. Make the blocks, placing fabrics as shown.

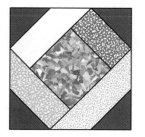

G41
Make 12.

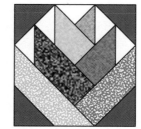

F73
1½" x 1½"
Make 13.

F73
1" x 1"
Make 4.

3. Sew the large Flower blocks (F73) and Geometric blocks (G41) in horizontal rows. Join the rows.

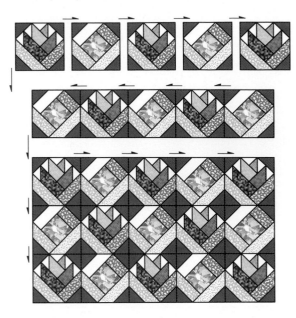

4. Sew black floral inner border strips to the sides of the quilt top. Add a small Flower block (F73) to each end of the remaining black floral inner border strips, then sew the strips to the top and bottom edges.

5. Sew 1½" x 10" black outer border strips to the sides of the quilt top. Add the remaining black outer border strips to the top and bottom edges.

6. Referring to "Finishing" on pages 90–94, layer your quilt top with batting and backing; baste. Quilt as desired and bind the edges.

Creative Options

I played with different arrangements for these blocks and found two alternate quilt settings. You may discover even more.

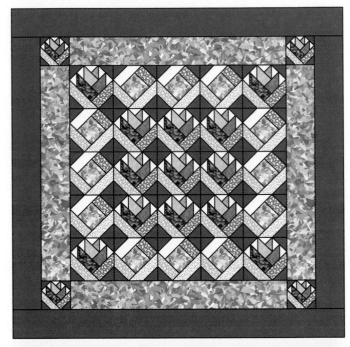

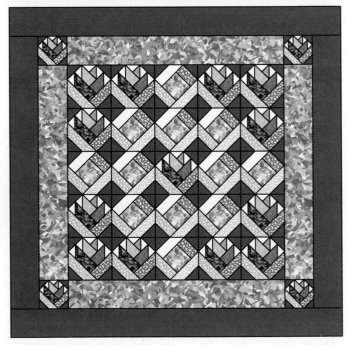

Jeweled Fans

Paper piecing allows you to make wonderfully sharp points, and the Fan block in this quilt takes advantage of that. Setting the Fan blocks on point creates an alternate block where the four corner triangles meet. I used the same fabrics in each Fan block, but the fan blades are perfect for a variety of scraps.

Materials

⅓ yd. navy blue for blocks, outer border, and binding
¼ yd. medium blue for blocks, pieced borders, and corner squares
¼ yd. light blue
⅛ yd. purple
⅛ yd. red
⅛ yd. green
¼ yd. pink for blocks and pieced borders
15" x 15" square of fabric for backing
15" x 15" square of batting

Navy blue   Medium blue   Light blue   Purple

Red   Green   Pink

1¾" x 1¾"

1¾" x 11"

Finished Quilt Size: 13" x 13"
Measurements in quilt plan are cut sizes.
Color photo on page 69.

PAPER-PIECING INFORMATION AT A GLANCE			
Paper-Pieced Units	Block/ Border No.	No. to Make	Finished Size of Unit
Large Geometric block	G42	16	2" x 2"
Small Geometric block	G42	4	1¼" x 1¼"
Pieced borders	PB4	4	1¼" x 8"

G42   PB4

Block-Front Drawings
Full-size patterns are on page 100.

Cutting Corner Squares, Borders and Binding

Fabric	No. of Pieces	Dimensions	Location
Navy blue	4	1¾" x 11"	Outer border
	1	1¾" x 40"	Binding
	1	1¾" x 20"	Binding
Medium blue	4	1¾" x 1¾"	Corner squares

Cutting for Blocks and Pieced Borders

Fabric	No. of Pieces	Dimensions	Location Number	Block/Border
Navy blue	32	2¼" x 2¼" ◹	14–17	G42 (large)
Medium blue	20	1" x 2"	1	G42 (both sizes)
	4	1½" x 9"	1	PB4
Light blue	120	1" x 1¼"	3, 4, 7, 8, 11, 12	G42 (both sizes)
Purple	20	1" x 2"	2	G42 (both sizes)
	8	2" x 2" ◹	14–17	G42 (small)
Red	40	1" x 1¾"	5, 6	G42 (both sizes)
Green	40	1" x 1¾"	9, 10	G42 (both sizes)
Pink	8	1" x 9"	2, 3	PB4
	20	1" x 1½"	13	G42 (both sizes)

Directions

1. Make 5 copies of page 100. Cut out patterns on the dotted lines for:
   - 16 large Geometric blocks (G42)
   - 4 small Geometric blocks (G42)
   - 4 pieced borders (PB4)
2. Make the blocks, placing fabrics as shown.

G42
2" x 2"
Make 16.

G42
1¼" x 1¼"
Make 4.

3. Make the pieced borders, placing fabrics as shown.

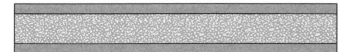

PB4
Make 4.

4. Sew the blocks into horizontal rows. Join the rows.

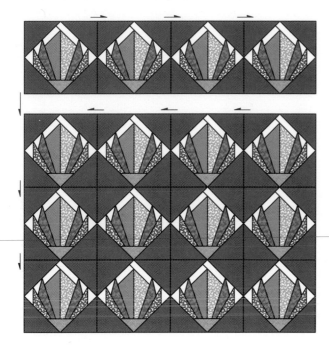

5. Sew pieced borders to the sides of the quilt top. Add a corner block to each end of the remaining pieced borders, then sew them to the top and bottom edges.

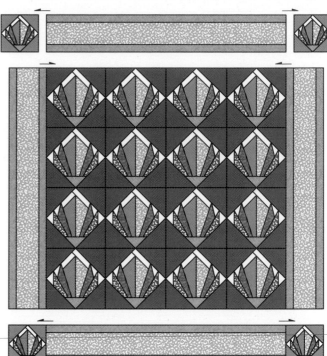

6. Sew 1¾" x 11" navy blue border strips to the sides of the quilt top. Add a medium blue corner square to each end of the remaining navy blue border strips, then sew the strips to the top and bottom edges of the quilt top.

7. Referring to "Finishing" on pages 90–94, layer your quilt top with batting and backing; baste. Quilt as desired and bind the edges.

Scrap Hearts

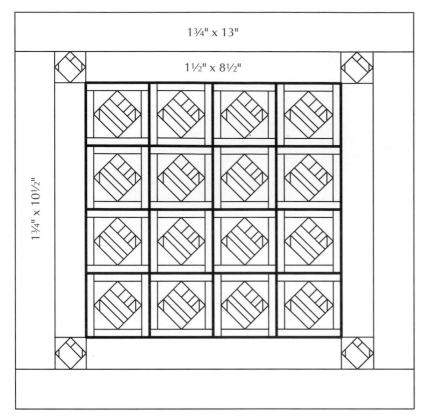

1¾" x 13"

1½" x 8½"

1¾" x 10½"

Finished Quilt Size: 12½" x 12½"
Measurements in quilt plan are cut sizes.
Color photo on page 71.

*T*his little heart quilt would be a perfect gift for someone special. The large Heart blocks contain six different randomly placed red fabrics, but feel free to use a variety of different colored fabrics to create a more intricate-looking quilt.

There are two large heart patterns. The only difference between them is the alternating side strips and the top and bottom strips. The strips eliminate the need to match seam intersections when joining the blocks.

Materials

¼ yd. of red #1 for blocks and outer border
¼ yd. of red #3 for blocks and binding
⅛ yd. *each* of reds #2, #4, #5, and #6
¼ yd. white
¼ yd. floral print for blocks and inner border
⅛ yd. blue
14" x 14" square of fabric for backing
14" x 14" square of batting

 Red #1   Red #2   Red #3

 Red #4   Red #5   Red #6

White   Floral print   Blue

PAPER-PIECING INFORMATION AT A GLANCE			
Paper-Pieced Units	Block/ Border No.	No. to Make	Finished Size of Unit
Large Heart blocks	H13	8	2" x 2"
Large Heart blocks	H14	8	2" x 2"
Small Heart blocks	H15	4	1" x 1"

H13   H14   H15

Block-Front Drawings
Full-size patterns are on page 101.

Cutting Borders and Binding

Fabric	No. of Pieces	Dimensions	Location
Red #1	2	1¾" x 10½"	Side outer borders
	2	1¾" x 13"	Top & bottom outer borders
Red #3	1	1¾" x 40"	Binding
	1	1¾" x 20"	Binding
Floral	4	1½" x 8½"	Inner border

Cutting for Blocks

Fabric	No. of Pieces	Dimensions	Location Number	Block
Reds #1, #4, #5, #6	16 each	1" x 1½"	2–4, 6–8	H13, H14*
Reds #2 and #3	20 each	1" x 1½"	2–4, 6–8	H13, H14*
			2, 4	H15
White	20	1" x 1"	1	H13, H14, H15
	16	1" x 2¾"	16, 17	H13, H14
	16	1" x 2"	14, 15	H13, H14
	10	2" x 2" ⊠	5, 9	H13, H14
			3, 5	H15
Floral	32	2" x 2" ◺	10–13	H13, H14
Blue	16	1" x 2¾"	16, 17	H13, H14
	16	1" x 2"	14, 15	H13, H14
	8	1¾" x 1¾" ◺	6–9	H15

*See step 2.

Directions

1. Make 3 copies of page 101. Cut out patterns on the dotted lines for:
   - 8 large Heart blocks (H13)
   - 8 large Heart blocks (H14)
   - 4 small Heart blocks (H15)
2. Make the blocks, placing the red fabrics randomly. (Use 1 of each red fabric in blocks H13 and H14.)

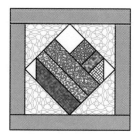

H13
Make 4.

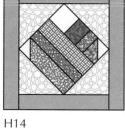

H14
Make 4.

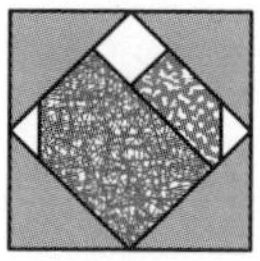

H15
Make 4.

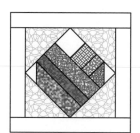

H13
Make 4.

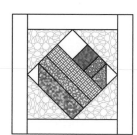

H14
Make 4.

3. Sew the H13 and H14 blocks into horizontal rows. Join the rows.

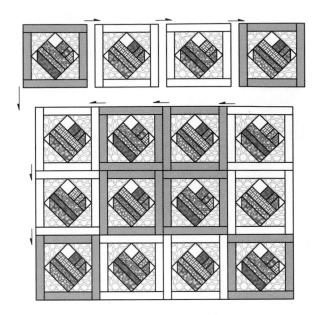

4. Sew floral inner border strips to the sides of the quilt top. Add a Heart block (H15) to each end of the remaining floral inner border strips, then sew them to the top and bottom edges of the quilt top.

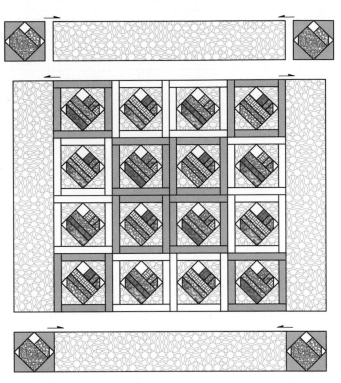

5. Sew 1¾" x 10½" red #1 border strips to the sides of the quilt top. Sew the remaining red #1 border strips to the top and bottom edges.
6. Referring to "Finishing" on pages 90–94, layer your quilt top with batting and backing; baste. Quilt as desired and bind the edges.

Tulips and Spools

My goal in designing this quilt was to create an alternating block quilt using a simple Geometric block. The snowball block with only five pieces was my first choice. When it was placed with a diagonally set Flower block, I saw the potential for creating a spool design at the intersecting corners. Adding the half-block designs around the perimeter completed the spool designs all the way to the edge.

The open area in the Snowball block is a good place to feature a quilting design. I machine quilted hearts and filled the shape with stipple quilting.

Materials

⅜ yd. light green for blocks, outer border, and binding
⅓ yd. white
⅛ yd. *each* peach #1 and peach #2
⅛ yd. *each* green #1 and green #2
⅓ yd. light peach
17½" x 17½" square of fabric for backing
17½" x 17½" square for batting

Light green   White   Peach #1   Peach #2

Green #1   Green #2   Light peach

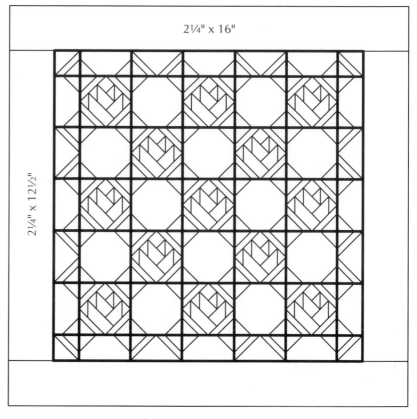

2¼" x 16"

2¼" x 12½"

Finished Quilt Size: 15½" x 15½"
Measurements in quilt plan are cut sizes.
Color photo on page 75.

PAPER-PIECING INFORMATION AT A GLANCE			
Paper-Pieced Units	Block/ Border No.	No. to Make	Finished Size of Unit
Flower block	F74	13	2" x 2"
Geometric block	G43	12	2" x 2"
Geometric block	G44	8	1" x 2"
Geometric block	G45	12	1" x 2"
Geometric block	G46	4	1" x 1"

   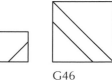

F74   G43   G44   G45   G46

Block-Front Drawings
Full-size patterns are on page 102.

		CUTTING BORDERS AND BINDING	
Fabric	No. of Pieces	Dimensions	Location
Light green	1	1¾" x 40"	Binding
	1	1¾" x 30"	Binding
	2	2¼" x 12½"	Side borders
	2	2¼" x 16"	Top and bottom borders

		CUTTING FOR BLOCKS		
Fabric	No. of Pieces	Dimensions	Location Number	Block
White	13	1" x 1"	1	F74
	13	2¼" x 2¼" ⊠	4, 5, 8, 9	F74
	12	2¾" x 2¾"	1	G43
	20	1¾" x 2¾"	1	G44, G45
	2	2¼" x 2¼" ◻	1	G46
Peach #1	4	2¼" x 2¼" ⊠	2	F74*
Peach #2	13	1" x 1½"	3	F74
Green #1	13	1" x 1½"	6	F74
Green #2	13	1" x 2"	7	F74
Light green	72	¾" x 3"	10–13	F74
			2, 3	G44
			2	G46
Light peach	72	2" x 2" ◻	14–17	F74
			2–5	G43
			4, 5	G44
			2, 3	G45
			3	G46

You will have 3 extra triangles.

Directions

1. Make 5 copies of page 102. Cut out patterns on the dotted lines for:
   - 13 Flower blocks (F74)
   - 12 Geometric blocks (G43)
   - 8 Geometric blocks (G44)
   - 12 Geometric blocks (G45)
   - 4 Geometric blocks (G46).
2. Make the blocks, placing fabrics as shown.

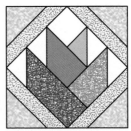

F74
Make 13.

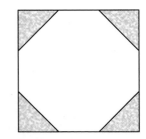

G43
Make 12.

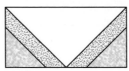

G44
Make 8.

G45
Make 12.

G46
Make 4.

3. Sew the blocks into horizontal rows. Press the seam allowances toward blocks G43 and G45. Join the rows.

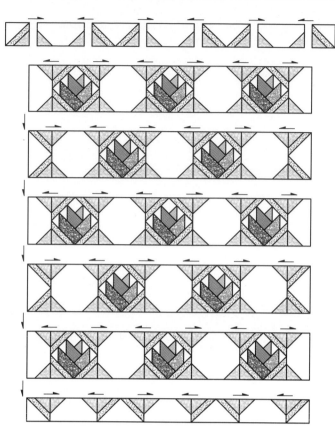

4. Sew 2¼" x 12½" light green border strips to the sides of the quilt top. Add the remaining light green border strips to the top and bottom edges.

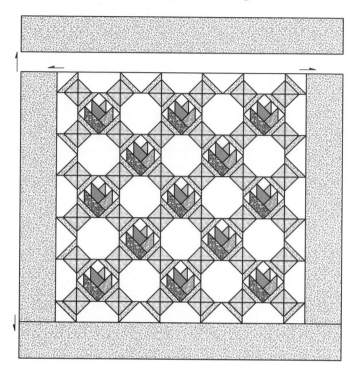

5. Referring to "Finishing" on pages 90–94, layer your quilt top with batting and backing; baste. Quilt as desired and bind the edges.

Simply Spools

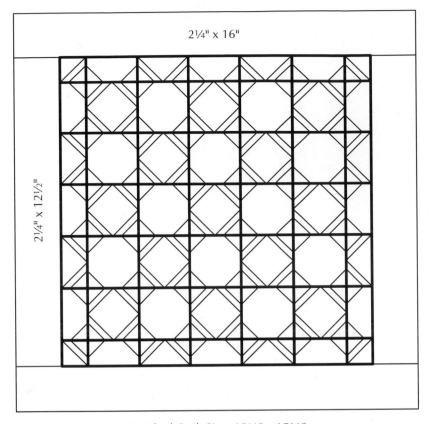

2¼" x 16"

2¼" x 12½"

Finished Quilt Size: 15½" x 15½"
Measurements in quilt plan are cut sizes.
Color photo on page 75.

After making "Tulips and Spools" (page 41), it occurred to me that I could make an entire spool quilt by eliminating the flower portion of block F74. This quilt is an ideal friendship quilt for a group of quilters. A fabric exchange would a nice way to gather scraps for the spools.

The open areas that replaced the flowers are great places to feature quilting. Although there are few pieces in this quilt, placing fabrics correctly for the different spools does require concentration.

Materials

⅜ yd. gray for blocks, outer border, and binding
⅓ yd. black
36 assorted fabrics, each 3" x 5", for spools
17½" x 17½" square of fabric for backing
17½" x 17½" square of batting

Black   Gray   Assorted fabrics

F74   G43

G44   G45   G46

Block-Front Drawings
Full-size patterns are on page 102.

Paper-Piecing Information at a Glance			
Paper-Pieced Units	Block/ Border No.	No. to Make	Finished Size of Unit
Revised Flower block	F74	13	2" x 2"
Geometric block	G43	12	2" x 2"
Geometric block	G44	8	1" x 2"
Geometric block	G45	12	1" x 2"
Geometric block	G46	4	1" x 1"

Cutting Borders and Binding			
Fabric	No. of Pieces	Dimensions	Location
Gray	1	1¾" x 40"	Binding
	1	1¾" x 30"	Binding
	2	2¼" x 12½"	Side borders
	2	2¼" x 16"	Top and bottom borders

Fabric	No. of Pieces	Dimensions	Location Number	Block
Black	25	2¾" x 2¾"	1–9	F74
			1	G43
	20	1¾" x 2¾"	1	G44, G45
	2	2¼" x 2¼" ◻	1	G46
Gray	72	¾" x 3"	10–13	F74
			2, 3	G44
			2	G46
Assorted fabrics	2 from	2" x 2" ◻	14–17	F74*
	each fabric		2–5	G43*
			4, 5	G44*
			2, 3	G45*
			3	G46*

See placement instructions in step 4.

Directions

1. Make 5 copies of page 102. Cut out patterns on the dotted lines for:
   - 13 Revised Flower blocks (F74)
   - 12 Geometric blocks (G43)
   - 8 Geometric blocks (G44)
   - 12 Geometric blocks (G45)
   - 4 Geometric blocks (G46).

2. Make 13 Flower blocks (F74) through piece #13 as shown. Piece #1 will cover areas #1 through #9. Place piece #1 straight, not on point, so the fabric grain will match the alternating block. Add pieces #10, #11, #12, and #13 only.

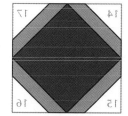

F74 pieced only through #13
Make 13.

3. Make the Geometric blocks, placing fabrics as shown and only through the numbers shown for each block.

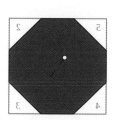

G43
Pin piece #1 in place.
Make 12.

G44 pieced only through #3
Make 8.

G46 pieced only through #2
Make 4.

G45
Pin piece #1 in place.
Make 12.

4. For the middle of the quilt, arrange the blocks made in steps 2 and 3 and the remainder of the paper patterns (blank side up). Select 4 triangles of one fabric. Sew 1 triangle in area #17 of the first F74 block in row one. Add the other 3 triangles to the blocks that meet at this corner. The scrap fabrics are textured in the illustration so you can see how they form spools at the corners. Continue adding triangles, using the same fabric at the corners, where the blocks meet.

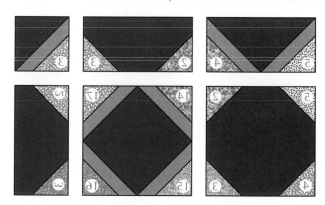

The upper left corner as seen from the blank side of the patterns.

5. Sew the blocks into horizontal rows, pressing the seam allowances toward blocks G43 and G45. Join the rows.

6. Sew 2¼" x 12½" gray border strips to the sides of the quilt top. Sew the remaining gray border strips to the top and bottom edges.

7. Referring to "Finishing" on pages 90–94, layer your quilt top with batting and backing; baste. Quilt as desired and bind the edges.

Tree of Life Medallion

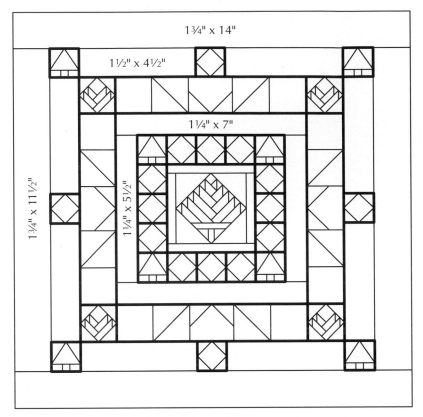

1¾" x 14"

1½" x 4½"

1¼" x 7"

1¾" x 11½"

1¼" x 5½"

Finished Quilt Size: 13½" x 13½"
Measurements in quilt plan are cut sizes.
Color photo on page 79.

This miniature quilt combines two of my favorite elements, the traditional Tree of Life pattern and medallion-style quilts. I centered fabric motifs in the sixteen Geometric blocks to add effortless detail to the middle of the quilt and to the border. Confirm that you can cut sixteen squares, centering the desired motif in area #1, from the suggested ⅛ yard. You may need a bit more, depending on the repeat of the desired motif in the fabric.

Materials

⅓ yd. navy blue for blocks, outer border, and binding
⅛ yd. dark blue for middle border
¼ yd. medium green
¼ yd. light blue
⅛ yd. blue focal print with motifs for sixteen 1½" squares
⅛ yd. brown
⅛ yd. dark green
⅛ yd. *total* assorted medium and light greens
15½" x 15½" square of fabric for backing
15½" x 15½" square of batting

Navy blue

Dark blue

Light blue

Blue print

Brown

Dark green

Medium green

Assorted medium and light green

Paper-Piecing Information at a Glance

Paper-Pieced Units	Block/ Border No.	No. to Make	Finished Size of Unit
Large Tree block	T15	1	3" x 3"
Small Tree block	T16	8	1" x 1"
Geometric block	G47	16	1" x 1"
Flower block	F75	4	1¼" x 1¼"
Pieced border	PB5	4	1¼" x 6½"

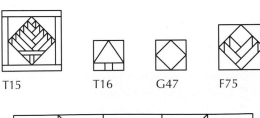

T15   T16   G47   F75

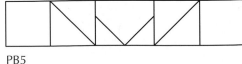

PB5

Block-Front Drawings
Full-size patterns are on page 103.

Cutting Borders and Binding

Fabric	No. of Pieces	Dimensions	Location
Navy blue	1	1¾" x 40"	Binding
	1	1¾" x 20"	Binding
	2	1¾" x 11½"	Side outer borders
	2	1¾" x 14"	Top & bottom outer borders
Dark blue	2	1¼" x 5½"	Side inner borders
	2	1¼" x 7"	Top & bottom inner borders
Medium green	8	1½" x 4½"	Middle border

Cutting for Blocks and Pieced Borders

Fabric	No. of Pieces	Dimensions	Location Number	Block/Border
Navy blue	4	1" x 4"	28–31	T15
	7	1" x 1"	1	T15 and F75
			23	T15*
	7	2" x 2" ⊠	4, 5, 8, 9, 12, 13	T15
			16, 17, 20, 21	T15
			4, 5, 8, 9	F75
Light blue	6	2½" x 2½" ◺	24–27	T15
			4, 7	PB5
	12	2" x 2"	1, 6, 9	PB5
	8	2" x 2" ◺	10–13	F75
	16	1" x 1"	2, 3	T16
	16	1" x 2"	5, 6	T16
Blue focal print	16	1½" x 1½"	1	G47**
Brown	9	1" x 1"	1	T16
			23	T15*
Dark green	4	2½" x 2½" ◺	5, 8	PB5
	4	2" x 2" ◺	2, 3	PB5
	8	1½" x 1½"	4	T16
Medium green	32	1¾" x 1¾" ◺	2–5	G47
Assorted medium & light greens	27	¾" x 2"	2, 3, 6, 7, 10, 11	T15
			14, 15, 18, 19, 22	T15
			2, 3, 6, 7	F75

*For pieced trunk unit.

**Center desired motif in square. See pages 11–12.

Directions

1. Make 4 copies of page 103. Cut out patterns on the dotted lines for:
   - 1 Tree block (T15)
   - 8 Tree blocks (T16)
   - 16 Geometric blocks (G47)
   - 4 Flower blocks (F75)
   - 4 pieced borders (PB5)
2. Make 1 large Tree block (T15), making piece #23 first. The hatch marks (//) on the trunk seam lines indicate that this is a pieced unit. Follow the steps below to join the 3 pieces.
   a. Position the brown fabric, right side up on the blank side of the paper, over the trunk area, as if it were piece #1. Sew 2 navy blue pieces to the trunk fabric as if they were pieces #2 and #3. Fold the paper back along the seam line that adjoins piece #22 and trim the pieced unit ⅛" from the fold. Place a piece of removable tape over the sewing lines. Carefully remove the pieced unit from the paper foundation and set it aside.
   b. When it is time to add pieced-unit #23, align the seam lines of the trunk with the trunk lines on the paper. Sew on the #22/#23 seam line, open the piece, pin the trunk straight, and press. Fold the paper back on line #24 and trim ⅛" from the fold.
   c. Machine baste a few stitches at the base of pieced-unit #23 to keep it straight and to keep it from moving as you add piece #24. Continue adding pieces, in order, to complete the block.

T15
Make 1.

3. Make the following blocks, placing fabrics as shown. To center a fabric motif in G47, see pages 11–12.

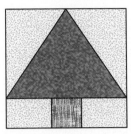

T16
Make 8.

G47
Make 16.

F75
Make 4.

4. Make the pieced borders, placing fabrics as shown.

PB5
Make 4.

5. Sew the 4 small trees (T16) and 12 Geometric blocks (G47) in rows as shown. Sew the rows to the center tree. Sew the 1¼" x 5½" dark blue inner border strips to the sides, then add the remaining dark blue inner border strips to the top and bottom edges. Press the seam allowance toward the inner borders.

6. Sew the pieced borders (PB5) to the sides. Add a Flower block (F75) to each end of the remaining pieced borders, then sew them to the top and bottom edges.

7. Sew a 1½" x 4½" medium green middle border strip to the sides of the remaining 4 Geometric blocks (G47). Sew 1 of these units to each side of the quilt top. Add a small Tree block (T16) to each end of the remaining units, then sew them to the top and bottom edges.

8. Sew a 1¾" x 11½" navy blue outer border strip to the sides of the quilt top. Sew the remaining navy blue outer border strips to the top and bottom edges.
9. Referring to "Finishing" on pages 90–94, layer your quilt top with batting and backing; baste. Quilt as desired and bind the edges.

Scrap Stars

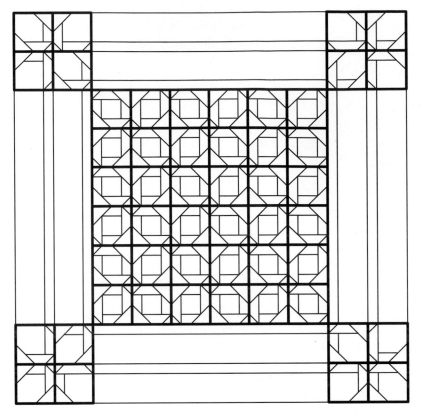

Finished Quilt Size: 12½" x 12½"
Color photo on page 65.

The simple Geometric block in this quilt creates an intriguing star design where the blocks meet. Combining variations of the Geometric block with pieced borders creates a unique border that mimics the center of the quilt. Cut several scraps of the same color family at once by layering fabrics when you cut your pieces.

Materials

½ yd. black for blocks, paper-pieced borders, and binding
⅛ yd. rose for blocks and paper-pieced border
⅛ yd. teal for blocks and paper-pieced border
¼ yd. *total* medium and light warm-color scraps
¼ yd. *total* medium and light cool-color scraps
14½" x 14½" square of fabric for backing
14½" x 14½" square of batting

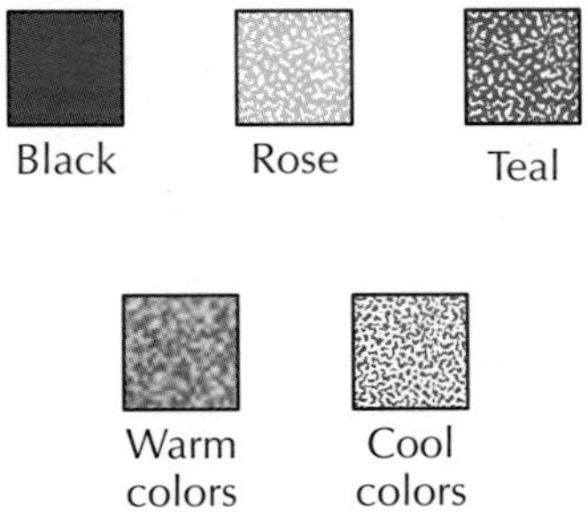

Black   Rose   Teal

Warm colors   Cool colors

PAPER-PIECING INFORMATION AT A GLANCE			
Paper-Pieced Units	Block/ Border No.	No. to Make	Finished Size of Unit
Geometric block	G48	36	1¼" x 1¼"
Geometric block	G49	8	1¼" x 1¼"
Geometric block	G50	4	1¼" x 1¼"
Geometric block	G51	4	1¼" x 1¼"
Pieced border	PB6	4	2½" x 7½"

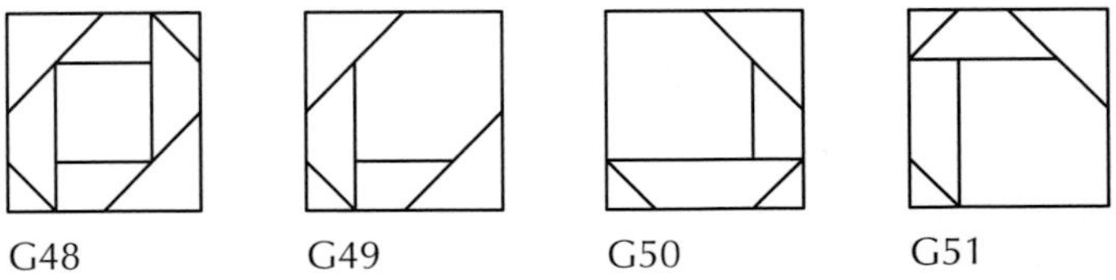

G48   G49   G50   G51

Block-Front Drawings
Full-size patterns are on page 104.

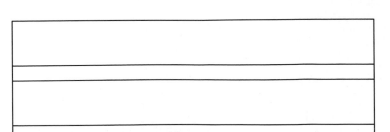

PB6

50

CUTTING FOR BINDING			
Fabric	No. of Pieces	Dimensions	Location
Black	1	1¾" x 40"	Binding
	1	1¾" x 20"	Binding

CUTTING FOR BLOCKS AND PIECED BORDERS			
Fabric	No. of Pieces	Dimensions	Location Number	Block/Border
Black	8	1½" x 8"	1, 4	PB6
	4	1½" x 1½" ◹	6	G50
			5	G51
	48	2" x 2" ◹	6, 7	G48
			4, 5	G49
			4	G50, G51
	16	1½" x 1½"	1	G49, G50, G51
	36	1" x 1"	1	G48
Rose	4	1" x 8"	2	PB6
Teal	4	1" x 8"	3	PB6
Warm colors	92	1" x 1½"	2, 5	G48
			2, 3	G49 (only 4)
			2	G50
			2, 3	G51
	4	1" x 2"	3	G50
	20	1½" x 1½" ◹	8	G48
			6	G49 (only 4)
Cool colors	80	1" x 1½"	3, 4	G48
			2, 3	G49 (only 4)
	24	1½" x 1½" ◹	9	G48
			6	G49 (only 4)
			5	G50
			6	G51

Directions

1. Make 6 copies of page 104. Cut out patterns on the dotted line, or cut ⅜" from the solid outer line of patterns without dotted lines, for:
   - 36 Geometric blocks (G48)
   - 8 Geometric blocks (G49)
   - 4 Geometric blocks (G50)
   - 4 Geometric blocks (G51)
   - 4 pieced borders (PB6)
2. Make the blocks, placing fabrics as shown.

G48
Make 36.

G49
Make 4.

G49
Make 4.

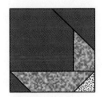

G50
Make 4.

G51
Make 4.

3. Make the pieced borders, placing fabrics as shown.

PB6
Make 4.

4. Sew the 36 Geometric blocks (G48) into horizontal rows as shown. Rotate the blocks as necessary to create warm and cool stars. Join the rows.

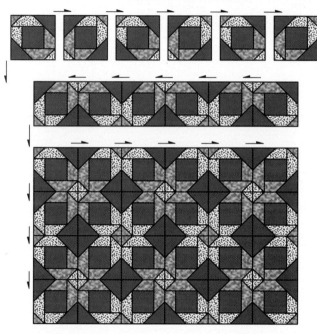

5. Join two G49 blocks—one of each color combination—one G50 block, and one G51 block as shown to make a corner unit.

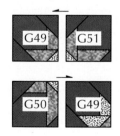 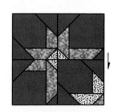

Make 4.

6. Sew pieced borders to the sides of the joined Geometric blocks. Add a corner unit to each end of the remaining pieced borders, then sew them to the top and bottom edges.

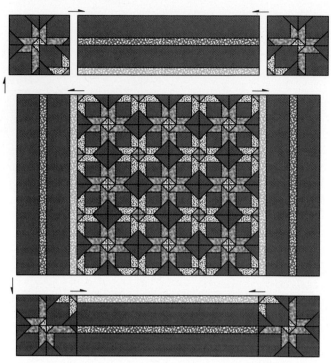

7. Referring to "Finishing" on pages 90–94, layer your quilt top with batting and backing; baste. Quilt as desired and bind the edges.

Spinning Stars

*T*here's lots of room for creativity when deciding where to place fabrics in this design. I chose a dark background and light and medium shades of blue and purple for the stars. For the blocks, I grouped like colors in a diamond around the central star to create a medallion-style setting. Pieced triangle units in the borders continue the medallion. Pieced corner squares continue the accent colors in the border.

There are quite a few blocks in this quilt, but the good news is that each has relatively few pieces.

Materials

½ yd. navy blue for the blocks, borders, and binding
⅛ yd. light blue
¼ yd. medium blue
¼ yd. light purple
⅛ yd. medium purple
13½" x 13½" square of fabric for backing
13½" x 13½" square of batting

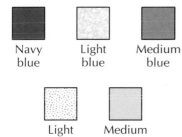

Navy blue	Light blue	Medium blue

Light purple	Medium purple

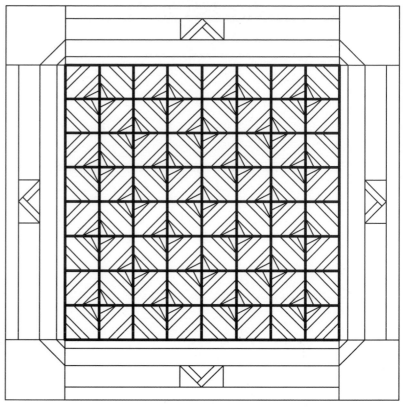

Finished Quilt Size: 11½" x 11½"
Color photo on page 67.

PAPER-PIECING INFORMATION AT A GLANCE			
Paper-Pieced Units	Block/ Border No.	No. to Make	Finished Size of Unit
Geometric block	G52	36	1" x 1"
Geometric block	G53	28	1" x 1"
Geometric block	G54	4	1¾" x 1¾"
Pieced border	PB7	4	1¾" x 8"

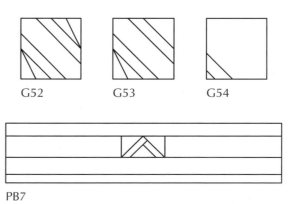

G52   G53   G54

PB7

Block-Front Drawings
Full-size patterns are on page 105.

Fabric	No. of Pieces	Dimensions	Location
Navy blue	1	1¾" x 40"	Binding
	1	1¾" x 15"	Binding

CUTTING FOR BLOCKS AND PIECED BORDERS

Fabric	No. of Pieces	Dimensions	Location Number	Block/Border
Navy blue	14	1¾" x 1¾" ◺	4	G53
	4	1" x 9"	10	PB7
	8	1¼" x 4"	6, 7	PB7
	64	1" x 2½"	1	G52, G53
	100	¾" x 1½"	4, 6	G52
			5	G53
	4	2½" x 2½"	1	G54
	4	2" x 2" ◺	4, 5	PB7
Light blue	48	1" x 1½"	7	G52*
			5, 7	G52*
			6	G53*
Medium blue	4	1" x 9"	9	PB7
	76	¾" x 2¼"	2	G52*
			2, 3	G52*
			2, 3	G53*
			2	G53*
	2	1½" x 1½" ◺	3	G54
	1	2¼" x 2¼" ⊠	1	PB7
Light purple	4	1¼" x 9"	8	PB7
	52	1" x 1½"	5	G52*
			5, 7	G52*
			6	G53*
	4	¾" x 2½"	2	G54
Medium purple	52	¾" x 2¼"	3	G52*
			2, 3	G52*
			3	G53*
	8	1" x 1½"	2, 3	PB7

*See step 2.

Directions

1. Make 6 copies of page 105. Cut out patterns on the dotted lines, or cut ⅜" from the solid outside line where there is no dotted line, for:

36 Geometric blocks (G52)
28 Geometric blocks (G53)
4 Geometric blocks (G54)
4 pieced borders (PB7)

2. Make the blocks, placing fabrics as shown.

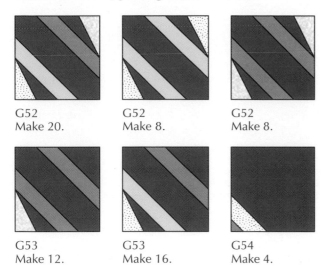

G52
Make 20.

G52
Make 8.

G52
Make 8.

G53
Make 12.

G53
Make 16.

G54
Make 4.

3. Make the pieced borders, placing fabrics as shown.

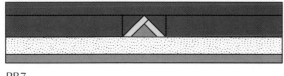

PB7
Make 4.

4. Sew the blocks (except G54) into horizontal rows. Join the rows.

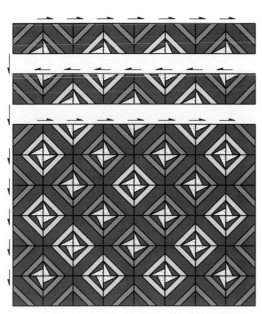

5. Sew pieced borders to the sides of the quilt top. Add a Geometric block (G54) to each end of the remaining pieced borders, then sew them to the top and bottom edges.

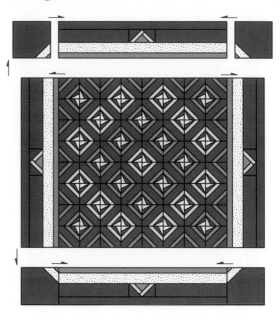

6. Referring to "Finishing" on pages 90–94, layer your quilt top with batting and backing; baste. Quilt as desired and bind the edges.

Creative Option

Place different fabrics in opposite corners of block G52 to create an alternate quilt design.

 Use block G52 to create the following quilt design.

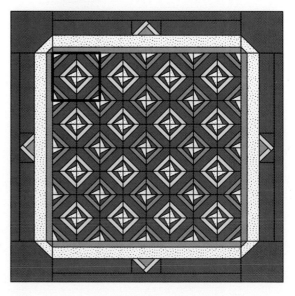

Rain Bonnet Sue

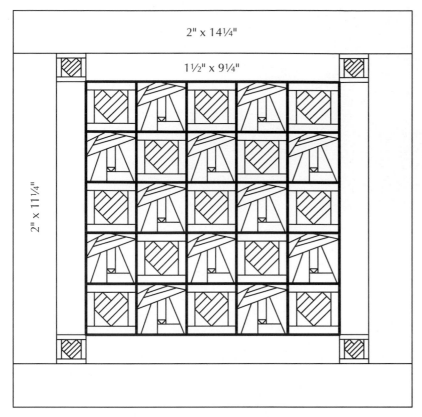

2" x 14¼"

1½" x 9¼"

2" x 11¼"

Finished Quilt Size: 13¾" x 13¾"
Measurements in quilt plan are cut sizes.
Color photo on page 76.

This quilt features alternating Rain Bonnet Sue and framed Heart blocks. The hearts' rainbow colors suggest that the sun has come out after a downpour. I used the same fabrics in each of the Rain Bonnet Sue and Heart blocks; however, this quilt is an ideal candidate for scraps too. Another idea is to use scraps from outgrown clothing to make a memory quilt for a special little girl.

Materials

¼ yd. medium fuchsia for blocks (bonnet),
  outer border, and binding
⅓ yd. white for blocks, and inner border
¼ yd. light blue
⅛ yd. blue check (apron)
⅛ yd. dark blue (dress sleeve, small heart)
⅛ yd. medium blue (dress)
⅛ yd. dark fuchsia (bonnet)
⅛ yd. blue print (heart)
⅛ yd. yellow (heart)
⅛ yd. pink (heart)
⅛ yd. green (heart)
⅛ yd. lavender (heart)
16" x 16" square of fabric for backing
16" x 16" square of batting

PAPER-PIECING INFORMATION AT A GLANCE			
Paper-Pieced Units	Block/ Border No.	No. to Make	Finished Size of Unit
Picture block	P48	12	1¾" x 1¾"
Large Heart block	H16	13	1¾" x 1¾"
Small Heart block	H16	4	1" x 1"

P48   H16

Block-Front Drawings
Full-size patterns are on page 107.

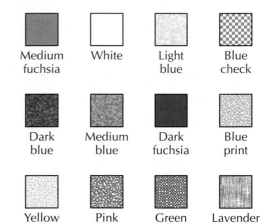

Medium fuchsia   White   Light blue   Blue check

Dark blue   Medium blue   Dark fuchsia   Blue print

Yellow   Pink   Green   Lavender

Cutting Borders and Binding

Fabric	No. of Pieces	Dimensions	Location
Medium fuchsia	1	1¾" x 40"	Binding
	1	1¾" x 25"	Binding
	2	2" x 14¼"	Top & bottom outer borders
	2	2" x 11¼"	Side outer borders
White	4	1½" x 9¼"	Inner border

Cutting for Blocks

Fabric	No. of Pieces	Dimensions	Location Number	Block
Light blue	24	1½" x 2"	8, 9	P48
	36	1" x 2"	13–15	P48
Blue check	12	1" x 1½"	5	P48*
Dark blue	28	¾" x 1½"	4	P48
			11–14	H16 (small)
Medium blue	24	1" x 2"	6, 7	P48
	12	1½" x 1½" ◺	2, 3	P48
Dark fuchsia	12	¾" x 2½"	10	P48
	12	¾" x 1½"	12	P48
Medium fuchsia	12	¾" x 2"	11	P48
White	26	1" x 2½"	13, 14	H16 (large)
	26	1" x 1¾"	11, 12	H16 (large)
	13	2" x 2" ◺	9, 10	H16 (large)
	8	2" x 2" ⊠	3	H16 (both)
			1	P48
	21	1½" x 1½" ◺	7, 8	H16 (both)
			9, 10	H16 (small)
Blue print	17	¾" x 1"	2	H16 (both)
Yellow	17	¾" x 1"	1	H16 (both)
Pink	17	¾" x 1½"	4	H16 (both)
Green	17	¾" x 1½"	5	H16 (both)
Lavender	17	¾" x 1½"	6	H16 (both)

Be sure to cut parallel to the check in the fabric.

Directions

1. Make 3 copies of page 107. Cut out patterns on the dotted lines for:
    - 12 Picture blocks (P48)
    - 13 large Heart blocks (H16)
    - 4 small Heart blocks (H16)
2. Make the blocks, placing fabrics as shown.

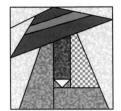

P48
Make 12.

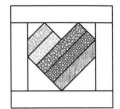

H16
1¾" x 1¾"
Make 13.

H16
1" x 1"
Make 4.

3. Sew the blocks into horizontal rows. Press the seam allowances toward the Heart block. Join the rows.

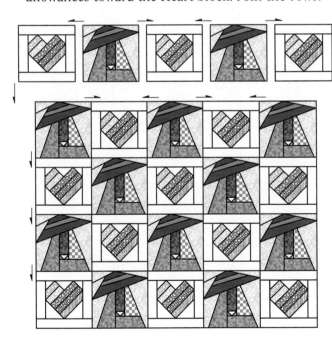

4. Sew white inner border strips to the sides of the quilt top. Add a small Heart block (H16) to each end of the remaining white inner border strips, then sew them to the top and bottom edges.

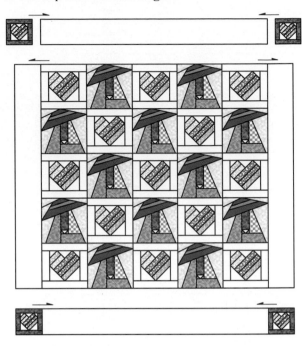

5. Sew 2" x 11¼" medium fuchsia outer border strips to the sides of the quilt top. Sew the remaining medium fuchsia outer border strips to the top and bottom edges.
6. Referring to "Finishing" on pages 90–94, layer your quilt top with batting and backing; baste. Quilt as desired and bind the edges.

Creative Option

Here's another setting for these blocks.

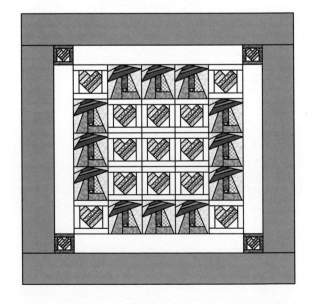

Shade Trees

This elegant yet simple design features Tree blocks in two sizes. The medallion setting creates design impact and the greens and restful blue and white fabrics provide simplicity. If your scrap basket overflows with green fabrics, this quilt would be the perfect place to use them.

Materials

⅛ yd. green #1 (darkest)
¼ yd. green #2 for blocks, outer border, and binding
⅛ yd. green #3
⅛ yd. green #4
⅛ yd. green #5 (lightest)
⅜ yd. medium blue for blocks and middle border
¼ yd. white for blocks and inner border
¼ yd. gray
16" x 16" square of fabric for backing
16" x 16" square of batting

| Green #1 (darkest) | Green #2 | Green #3 | Green #4 |

| Green #5 (lightest) | Medium blue | White | Gray |

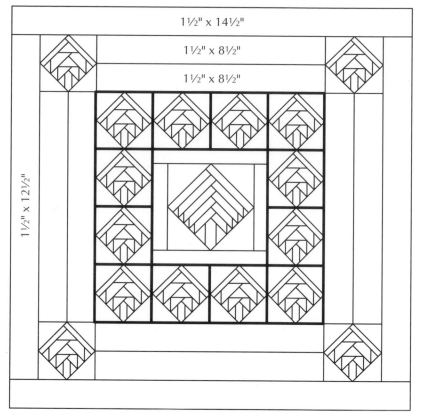

1½" x 14½"
1½" x 8½"
1½" x 8½"
1½" x 12½"

Finished Quilt Size: 14" x 14"
Measurements in quilt plan are cut sizes.
Color photo on page 78.

PAPER-PIECING INFORMATION AT A GLANCE			
Paper-Pieced Units	Block/ Border No.	No. to Make	Finished Size of Unit
Small Tree block	T17	16	2" x 2"
Large Tree block	T18	1	4" x 4"

T17   T18

Block-Front Drawings
Full-size patterns are on page 109.

CUTTING BORDERS AND BINDING

Fabric	No. of Pieces	Dimensions	Location
Green 2	1	1¾" x 40"	Binding
	1	1¾" x 25"	Binding
	2	1½" x 12½"	Side outer border
	2	1½" x 14½"	Top and bottom outer border
Medium blue	4	1½" x 8½"	Middle border
White	4	1½" x 8½"	Inner border

CUTTING FOR BLOCKS

Fabric	No. of Pieces	Dimensions	Location Number	Block
Green 1	16	¾" x 1½"	1	T17
	1	1" x 1¾"	1	T18
Green 2	2	¾" x 2½"	16, 17	T18
	16	1" x 1½"	9	T17
Green 3	2	¾" x 2¼"	12, 13	T18
	16	1" x 1¼"	6	T17
Green 4	2	¾" x 2"	8, 9	T18
	32	1" x 1¼"	5, 11	T17
Green 5	2	¾" x 1½"	4, 5	T18
	32	1" x 1½"	4, 10	T17
Gray	27	2" x 2" ⊠	2, 3, 7, 8, 12, 13	T17
			2, 3, 6, 7, 10, 11	T18
			14, 15, 18, 19	T18
	32	¾" x 2"	14, 15	T17
	2	¾" x 2½"	20, 21	T18
Medium blue	2	2¾" x 2¾" ◳	22–25	T18
	30	2¼" x 2¼" ◳	16–19	T17
White	2	2¼" x 2¼" ◳	16–19	T17*
	4	1" x 4¾"	26–29	T18

Used in only 1 corner in each of the 4 corner blocks. See step 2.

Directions

1. Make 4 copies of page 109. Cut out patterns on the dotted lines, or cut ⅜" from the solid outside line where there is no dotted line, for:
   - 1 Tree block (T18)
   - 16 Tree blocks (T17)
2. Make the blocks, placing fabrics as shown.

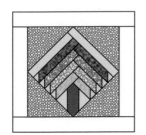

T18
Make 1.

T17
Make 12.

T17
Make 1.

T17
Make 1.

T17
Make 1.

T17
Make 1.

3. Sew the 12 identical small Tree blocks (T17) to the large Tree block (T18) as shown.

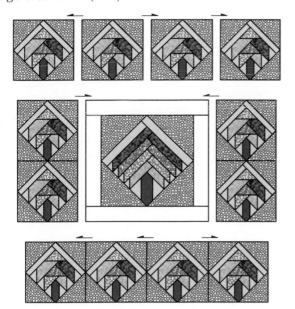

4. Sew each light blue border strip to a white border strip as shown.

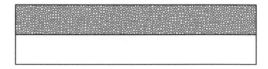

Make 4.

5. Sew a pieced border to the sides of the unit made in step 3. Add a small Tree block (T17) to each end of the remaining pieced borders, then sew them to the top and bottom edges.

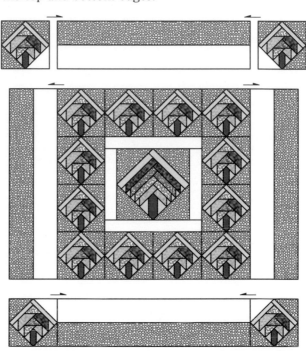

6. Sew 1½" x 12½" green #2 outer border strips to the sides of the quilt top. Sew the remaining outer border strips to the top and bottom edges.
7. Referring to "Finishing" on pages 90–94, layer your quilt top with batting and backing; baste. Quilt as desired and bind the edges.

My Little Town

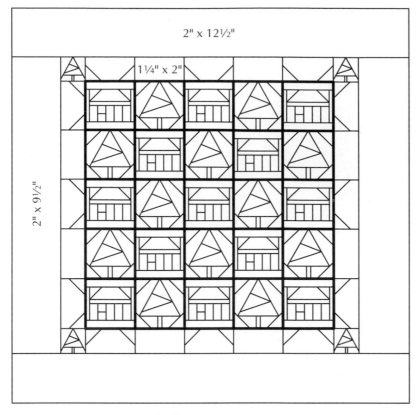

2" x 12½"

1¼" x 2"

2" x 9½"

Finished Quilt Size: 12" x 12"
Measurements in quilt plan are cut sizes.
Color photo on page 70.

I've always loved pieced houses and trees. This little quilt gave me the chance to use a lot of scraps. Remember, these houses are tiny, so use small-scale prints. Layer the fabrics for the houses to cut multiple pieces at once.

Materials

⅜ yd. dark red for blocks, border, and binding
⅓ yd. light blue
⅛ yd. dark green
⅛ yd. medium green
⅛ yd. light green
⅛ yd. black for roofs and trunks
⅛ yd. yellow for windows
13 assorted scrap fabrics, each 1" x 6", for the houses
14" x 14" square of fabric for backing
14" x 14" square of batting

 Dark red

 Light blue

 Dark green

 Medium green

 Light green

 Black

 Yellow

Assorted scraps

PAPER-PIECING INFORMATION AT A GLANCE			
Paper-Pieced Units	Block/ Border No.	No. to Make	Finished Size of Unit
Picture block	P49	13	1½" x 1½"
Large Tree block	T19	12	1½" x 1½"
Small Tree block	T20	4	¾" x ¾"
Geometric half block	G55	12	1½" x ¾"

 P49

 T19

 T20

 G55

Block-Front Drawings
Full-size patterns are on page 106.

Fabric	No. of Pieces	Dimensions	Location
Light blue	8	1¼" x 2"	Pieced border
Dark red	1	1¾" x 40"	Binding
	1	1¾" x 20"	Binding
	2	2" x 9½"	Side border
	2	2" x 12½"	Top and bottom border

CUTTING FOR BLOCKS

Fabric	No. of Pieces	Dimensions	Location Number	Block
Light blue	39	¾" x 2¼"	11–13	P49
	13	1¾" x 1¾" ◊	9, 10	P49
	24	1" x 2"	7, 8	T19
	32	1" x 1"	2, 3	T19, T20
	8	1" x 1½"	7, 8	T20
	12	1½" x 2¼"	1	G55
Dark red	36	1¾" x 1¾" ◊	9–12	T19
			2, 3	G55
	13	¾" x 1"	5	P49
Dark green	12	1" x 1½"	5	T19
	4	1" x ¾"	5	T20
	13	¾" x 2¼"	14	P49
Medium green	12	1" x 2"	4	T19
	4	1" x ¾"	4	T20
Light green	12	1" x 1½"	6	T19
	4	1" x ¾"	6	T20
Black	13	1" x 2"	8	P49
	16	1" x ¾"	1	T19, T20
Yellow	13	1" x ¾"	1	P49
Assorted scraps	4 from each	¾" x 1"	2–4, 6	P49
	1 from each	¾" x 1¾"	7	P49

Directions

1. Make 5 copies of page 106. Cut out patterns on the dotted lines for:
   - 13 Picture blocks (P49)
   - 12 Tree blocks (T19)
   - 4 Tree blocks (T20)
   - 12 Geometric half blocks (G55)
2. Make the blocks, placing fabrics as shown.

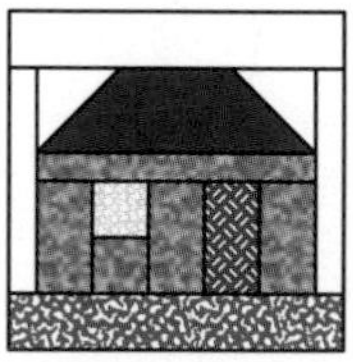

P49
Make 13.

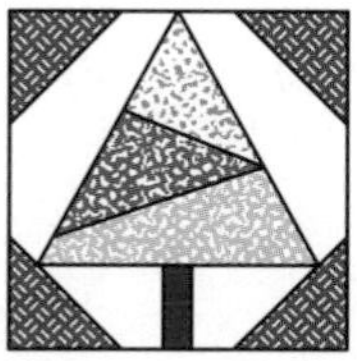

T19
Make 12.

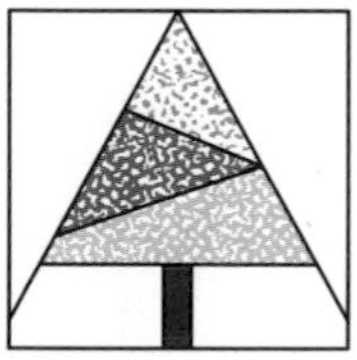

T20
Make 4.

G55
Make 12.

3. Sew blocks P49 and T19 into horizontal rows as shown. Press the seam allowances toward the large Tree blocks (T19). Join the rows.

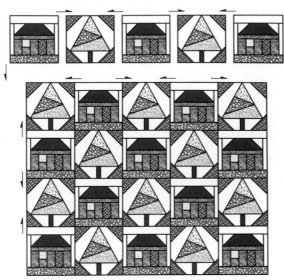

4. Join two 1¼" x 2" light blue rectangles and the three Geometric half blocks (G55) to make a pieced border. Make a total of 4 pieced borders.

5. Sew pieced borders to the sides of the quilt top. Add a small Tree block (T20) to each end of the remaining pieced borders as shown, then sew them to the top and bottom edges.

6. Sew 2" x 9½" dark red border strips to the sides of the quilt top. Sew the remaining dark red border strips to the top and bottom edges.

7. Referring to "Finishing" on pages 90–94, layer your quilt top with batting and backing; baste. Quilt as desired and bind the edges.

Creative Options

The same block designs can be used in other settings. The following settings require fewer pieced blocks. To create the Snowball block in the second option, simply place a piece of light blue fabric over the center portion of the Tree block (pieces #1–#8) and begin piecing with triangle #9.

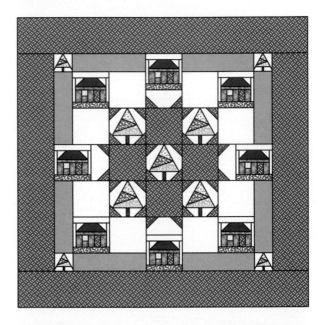

GALLERY

SCRAP STARS

by Carol Doak, 1996, Windham,
New Hampshire, 12½" x 12½".

I love the variety of the warm and cool
scrap fabrics. Each star is a combination
of four simple Geometric blocks. The corner
squares in the borders are variations
of the Geometric block.
Directions begin on page 50.

MARINER'S COMPASS

by Carol Doak, 1996, Windham,
New Hampshire, 10" x 10".

Intricate piecing in the middle of this quilt
grabs your attention. Soothing blue and
lavender scraps suggest a nautical theme.
Directions begin on page 29.

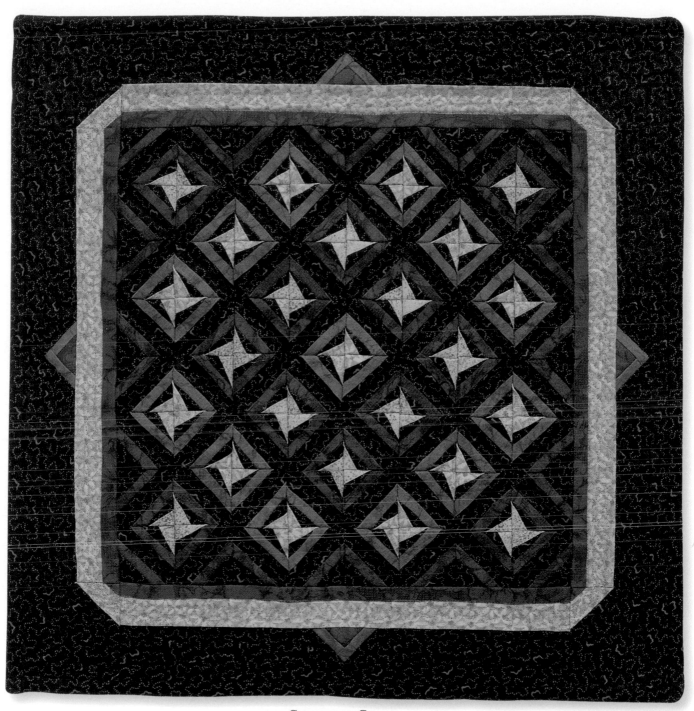

SPINNING STARS

by Carol Doak, 1997, Windham,
New Hampshire, 11½" x 11½".

Just two blocks make up the middle of this
quilt, but changing colors form a medallion
design. The coordinated paper-pieced border
continues the medallion theme.
Directions begin on page 53.

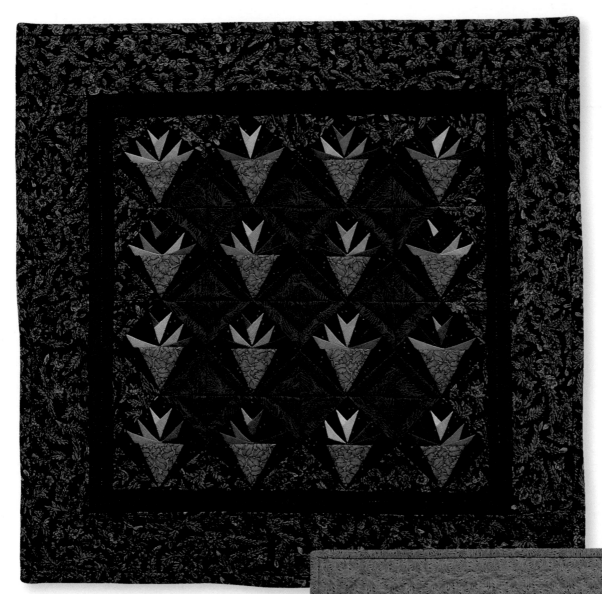

LITTLE NOSEGAYS

by Carol Doak, 1996, Windham,
New Hampshire, 11½" x 11½".

Although this quilt appears to be made up of
alternating blocks, it isn't. The solids in the
nosegay sparkle against a dark background.
Directions begin on page 26.

LITTLE GREEN NOSEGAYS

by Carol Doak, 1996, Windham,
New Hampshire, 11½" x 11½".

Soft pastels give the Nosegay
quilt an antique look.

JEWELED FANS

by Carol Doak, 1996, Windham,
New Hampshire, 13" x 13".

Fan blocks feature vivid jewel
tones set against soft blue. Notice the decorative
stitches machine quilted in the borders.
Directions begin on page 35.

My Little Town

*by Carol Doak, 1997, Windham,
New Hampshire, 12" x 12".*

Making the little House block was like
making doll houses. After finishing one
house, I couldn't wait to see how each
fabric would look in the next.
Directions begin on page 62.

SCRAP HEARTS

by Carol Doak, 1996, Windham,
New Hampshire, 12½" x 12½".

The tiny-scale print sets a country
theme, and red fabrics provide variety.
The bit of blue surrounding the hearts
focuses attention there.
Directions begin on page 38.

FLOWER TRELLIS

by Carol Doak, 1996, Windham,
New Hampshire, 11½" x 11½".

The Geometric blocks and borders feature
a rich floral fabric. A touch of gold in the
quilting continues the elegant theme.
Directions begin on page 32.

AMISH BASKETS

*by Carol Doak, 1996, Windham,
New Hampshire, 11" x 11".*

The on-point basket is the perfect place
to feature a bouquet of flowers.
Directions begin on page 23.

BEIGE AMISH BASKETS

*by Carol Doak, 1996, Windham,
New Hampshire, 11" x 11".*

Soft beige, country red, and green
create a country look.

LOG CABIN GARDEN

by Carol Doak, 1997, Windham,
New Hampshire, 13" x 13".

This quilt uses a simple Flower block in a
medallion-style setting for a dramatic effect.
The paper-pieced border continues the theme.
Directions begin on page 84.

TULIPS AND SPOOLS

by Carol Doak, 1996, Windham, New Hampshire, 15½" x 15½".

At first glance, the Tulip blocks catch your eye, but a second look reveals spools between the tulips. The alternating Geometric block is the perfect place to do a "little" quilting.
Directions begin on page 41.

SIMPLY SPOOLS

by Virginia Guaraldi, 1997, Londonderry, New Hampshire, 15½" x 15½".

This simplified version of "Tulips and Spools" features a variety of spool colors, sparkling against a black background.
Directions begin on page 44.

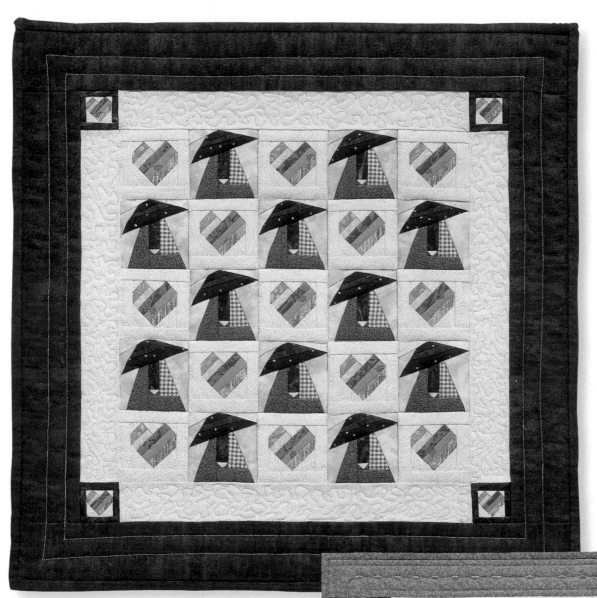

RAIN BONNET SUE

by Carol Doak, 1997, Windham,
New Hampshire, 13¾" x 13¾".

I had such fun making this little gal!
The rainbow strips in the Heart blocks
suggest the sun is about to come out.
Directions begin on page 56.

FLYING NUNS QUILT

Terry Maddox, 1997, Pelham,
New Hampshire, 13¾" x 13¾".

Terry's parochial school memories
inspired flying Nuns rather than little girls.
She claimed that she had a bit of divine
guidance as she skillfully machine quilted
an accurate rosary around the border.

COUNTRY BASKETS

by Carol Doak, 1997, Windham,
New Hampshire, 11" x 11".

Since miniatures make ideal gift quilts,
I set out to design one that would be quick
to make. The alternating Geometric blocks
feature flowers, creating the illusion of a star
in the center. However, another motif
could reflect a different theme.
Directions begin on page 87.

SHADE TREES

by Carol Doak, 1997, Windham,
New Hampshire, 14" x 14".

Cool green and blue fabrics give this
medallion-style quilt a restful feeling.
Autumn-colored fabrics could
represent a different season.
Directions begin on page 59.

TREE OF LIFE MEDALLION

by Carol Doak, 1996, Windham,
New Hampshire, 13½" x 13½".

Even I was surprised by the impact of the centered fabric motifs in the Geometric blocks. The
paper-pieced border is easy to make, yet dramatic.
Directions begin on page 46.

CHRISTMAS BELLS MEDALLION

by Sherry Reis, 1997, Worthington, Ohio,
13½" x 13½".

Red and green fabrics and a bell motif in the
Geometric blocks turn "Tree of Life Medallion"
into a charming Christmas quilt. It's perfect
for the holidays, but this quilt could be
displayed year 'round.

SIMPLY SOLIDS

*by Carol Doak, 1997, Windham,
New Hampshire, 12" x 12".*

Since solid fabrics are so dramatic in
miniature quilts, I designed this simple
Geometric block to feature them. The
Amish-style setting is just one of many
design possibilities for this block.
Directions begin on the facing page.

Simply Solids

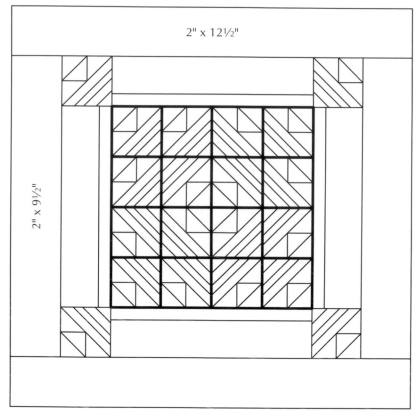

2" x 12½"

2" x 9½"

Finished Quilt Size: 12" x 12"
Measurements in quilt plan are cut sizes.
Color photo on facing page.

Since I'd been using a lot of prints in my miniature quilts, I decided to design a simple Geometric block and use only solid fabrics. I used the same fabric placement in each block and arranged the blocks in a setting typical of an Amish-style Square within a Square quilt. Did you notice that not all the seams in the strips match, but they look as though they do?

Materials

¼ yd. purple for blocks, outer border, and binding
¼ yd. black
⅛ yd. light pink
⅛ yd. blue
⅛ yd. light turquoise
⅛ yd. dark turquoise
⅛ yd. dark pink
14" x 14" square of fabric for backing
14" x 14" square of batting

Purple   Black   Light pink   Blue

Light turquoise   Dark turquoise   Dark pink

PAPER-PIECING INFORMATION AT A GLANCE			
Paper-Pieced Units	Block/ Border No.	No. to Make	Finished Size of Unit
Geometric block	G56	20	1½" x 1½"
Pieced border	PB10	4	1½" x 6"

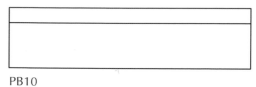

G56   PB10

Block-Front Drawings
Full-size patterns are on page 110.

Fabric	No. of Pieces	Dimensions	Location
Purple	1	1¾" x 40"	Binding
	1	1¾" x 20"	Binding
	2	2" x 9½"	Side borders
	2	2" x 12½"	Top & bottom borders

CUTTING FOR BLOCKS AND PIECED BORDERS

Fabric	No. of Pieces	Dimensions	Location Number	Block/Border
Black	20	2" x 2" ◻	3, 4	G56
	4	1¾" x 7"	1	PB10
Light pink	10	2" x 2" ◻	1	G56
Blue	10	2" x 2" ◻	2	G56
Light turquoise	4	1" x 7"	2	PB10
	20	¾" x 3"	5	G56
Dark turquoise	20	¾" x 2½"	6	G56
Purple	20	¾" x 2"	7	G56
Dark pink	10	1¾" x 1¾" ◻	8	G56

Directions

1. Make 4 copies of page 110. Cut out patterns on the dotted lines for:
   20 Geometric blocks (G56)
   4 pieced borders (PB10)
2. Make the blocks, placing fabrics as shown.

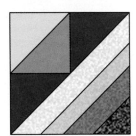

G56
Make 20.

3. Make the pieced borders, placing fabrics as shown.

PB10
Make 4.

4. Sew the blocks into horizontal rows as shown. Join the rows.

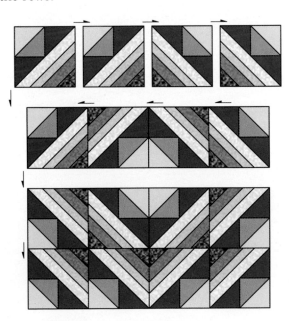

5. Sew pieced borders to the sides of the quilt top. Add a block to each end of the remaining pieced borders, then sew them to the top and bottom edges.

6. Sew a 2" x 9½" purple outer border strip to the sides of the quilt top. Sew the remaining purple outer border strips to the top and bottom edges.
7. Referring to "Finishing" on pages 90–94, layer your quilt top with batting and backing; baste. Quilt as desired and bind the edges.

Creative Options

The setting I used is only the beginning of the design possibilities for this easy block. I came up with two alternative settings. Play with the possibilities and see what you find.

Log Cabin Garden

1½" x 13½"

2" x 8½"

1½" x 11½"

Finished Quilt Size: 13" x 13"
Measurements in quilt plan are cut sizes.
Color photo on page 74.

*J*ust one block is used to create this medallion-style quilt. I rotated the four center blocks to create a radiating design. For the outer blocks, I changed the fabric in the large triangles to accentuate the center blocks. Although I used the same fabric placement in each Flower block, this quilt is another ideal candidate for scrap fabrics.

Materials

¼ yd. purple-and-green print for blocks, border, and binding
⅛ yd. green #1
⅛ yd. green #2 for blocks and middle border
⅛ yd. green #3
⅛ yd. green #4
⅓ yd. white
⅛ yd. dark pink
⅛ yd. purple #1
⅛ yd. purple #2
⅛ yd. purple #3
15" x 15" square of fabric for backing
15" x 15" square of batting

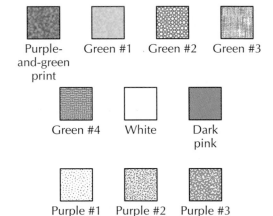

Purple-and-green print	Green #1	Green #2	Green #3
Green #4	White	Dark pink	
Purple #1	Purple #2	Purple #3	

PAPER-PIECING INFORMATION AT A GLANCE			
Paper-Pieced Units	Block/ Border No.	No. to Make	Finished Size of Unit
Flower block	F76	20	1½" x 1½"
Pieced border	PB8	2	1" x 6"
Pieced border	PB9	2	1" x 8"

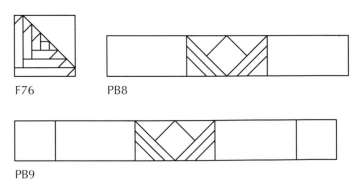

F76   PB8

PB9

Block-Front Drawings
Full-size patterns are on page 108.

Cutting Borders and Binding

Fabric	No. of Pieces	Dimensions	Location
Purple-and-green	1	1¾" x 40"	Binding
	1	1¾" x 20"	Binding
	2	1½" x 11½"	Side outer borders
	2	1½" x 13½"	Top bottom outer borders
Green #2	4	2" x 8½"	Middle border

Cutting for Blocks and Pieced Borders

Fabric	No. of Pieces	Dimensions	Location Number	Block/Border
Green #1	20	¾" x 1½"	8	F76
Green #2	4	1¾" x 1¾" ◻	8, 9	PB8, PB9
	20	¾" x 1¾"	9	F76
Green #3	28	¾" x 2"	12	F76
			6, 7	PB8, PB9
Green #4	28	¾" x 2¼"	13	F76
			4, 5	PB8, PB9
White	8	1¾" x 2¾"	10, 11	PB8, PB9
	4	2½" x 2½" ◻	16	F76
	2	2½" x 2½" ⊠	2, 3	PB8, PB9
	40	2" x 2" ⊠	2, 3, 6, 7, 10,	F76
			11, 14, 15	F76
Dark pink	4	1½" x 1½"	1	PB8, PB9
	20	¾" x 1"	1	F76
	4	1¾" x 1¾"	12, 13	PB9
Purple #1	6	2½" x 2½" ◻	16	F76
Purple #2	20	¾" x 1"	4	F76
Purple #3	20	¾" x 1¼"	5	F76

Directions

1. Make 4 copies of page 108. Cut out patterns on the dotted lines, or cut ⅜" from the solid outside line where there is no dotted line, for:
   - 20 Flower blocks (F76)
   - 2 pieced borders (PB8)
   - 2 pieced borders (PB9)
2. Make the blocks, placing fabrics as shown.

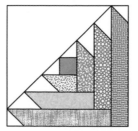

F76
Make 8.

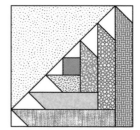

F76
Make 12.

3. Make the pieced borders, placing fabrics as shown.

PB8
Make 2.

PB9
Make 2.

4. Sew the Flower blocks into horizontal rows as shown. Join the rows.

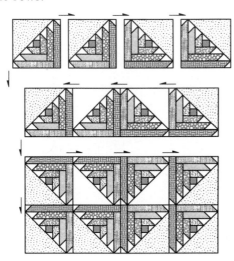

5. Sew pieced borders (PB8) to the sides of the quilt top. Sew the remaining pieced borders (PB9) to the top and bottom edges.

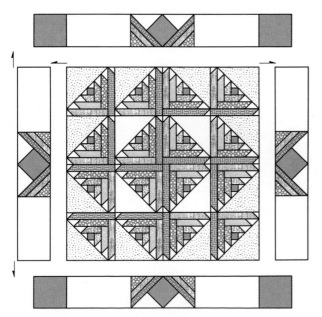

6. Sew a 2" x 8½" green #2 middle border strip to the sides of the quilt top. Add a Flower block to each end of the remaining green #2 middle border strips, then sew them to the top and bottom edges.

7. Sew 1½" x 11½" purple-and-green outer border strips to the sides of the quilt top. Sew the remaining purple-and-green outer border strips to the top and bottom edges.

8. Referring to "Finishing" on pages 90–94, layer your quilt top with batting and backing; baste. Quilt as desired and bind the edges.

Country Baskets

*S*ince miniature quilts make great gifts, I designed this project so that it could be made quickly. Centering a floral motif in the simple Geometric blocks allows you to add detail to your quilt without effort. I suggest you select your floral fabric first and coordinate the rest of your fabrics with it. Changing the color of the triangles in the blocks that surround the center square creates a radiating star, which gives the design impact of a medallion quilt.

This is a quick and easy project. You may find that you want to make two and keep one for yourself.

Materials

¼ yd. medium green for blocks, border, and binding
¼ yd. light green
⅛ yd. white fabric
⅛ yd. light pink
⅛ yd. medium pink
⅛ yd. blue check
⅛ yd. yellow
¼ yd. floral print with small motifs*
13" x 13" square of fabric for backing
13" x 13" square of batting

*You'll have extra yardage so you can center the motifs.

| Medium green | Light green | White | Light pink |
| Medium pink | Blue check | Yellow | Floral print |

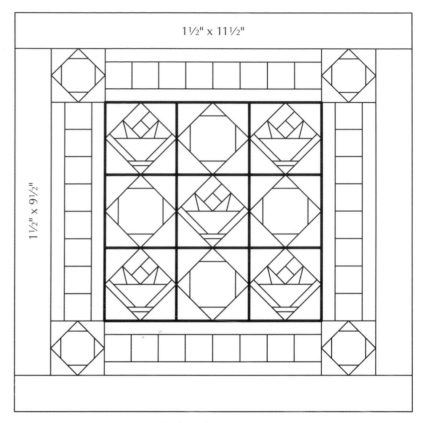

1½" x 11½"

1½" x 9½"

Finished Quilt Size: 11" x 11"
Measurements in quilt plan are cut sizes.
Color photo on page 77.

PAPER-PIECING INFORMATION AT A GLANCE

Paper-Pieced Units	Block/ Border No.	No. to Make	Finished Size of Unit
Basket block	B14	5	2" x 2"
Large Geometric block	G57	4	2" x 2"
Small Geometric block	G57	4	1½" x 1½"
Pieced border	PB11	4	1½" x 6"

  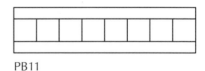

B14   G57   PB11

Block-Front Drawings
Full-size patterns are on page 111.

CUTTING BORDERS AND BINDING

Fabric	No. of Pieces	Dimensions	Location
Medium green	1	1¾" x 40"	Binding
	1	1¾" x 12"	Binding
	2	1½" x 9½"	Side borders
	2	1½" x 11½"	Top & bottom borders

CUTTING FOR BLOCKS AND PIECED BORDERS

Fabric	No. of Pieces	Dimensions	Location Number	Block/Border
Medium green	10	¾" x 1½"	4, 5	B14
	8	2" x 2" ⊠	2–5	G57 (both sizes)
	12	1½" x 1½"	1, 5, 8	PB11
Light green	12	2¼" x 2¼" ◻	13–16	B14 (4 blocks)
			6–9	G57 (large)*
	8	2" x 2" ◻	6–9	G57 (small)
	8	1½" x 1½"	3, 6	PB11
White	5	¾" x 1"	2	B14
	10	¾" x 1¼"	3, 12	B14
	10	¾" x 1¾"	9, 10	B14
	10	1¼" x 1¼"	6, 7	B14
Light pink	6	2¼" x 2¼" ◻	13–16	B14 (1 block)
			6–9	G57 (large)*
	4	1½" x 1½"	4	PB11
Medium pink	5	1" x ¾"	1	B14
	8	1½" x 1½"	2, 7	PB11
Blue check	5	1¼" x 2"	8	B14
	5	¾" x 1¼"	11	B14
Yellow	8	1" x 7"	9, 10	PB11
Floral	4	2" x 2"	1	G57 (large)**
	4	1½" x 1½"	1	G57 (small)**

*See step 2 for correct placement.

**Center motif in each square. See pages 11–12.

Directions

1. Make 4 copies of page 111. Cut out patterns on the dotted lines for:
   - 5 Basket blocks (B14)
   - 4 large Geometric blocks (G57)
   - 4 small Geometric blocks (G57)
   - 4 pieced borders (PB11)
2. Make the blocks, placing fabrics as shown.

B14
Make 4.

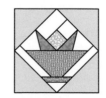

B14
Make 1.

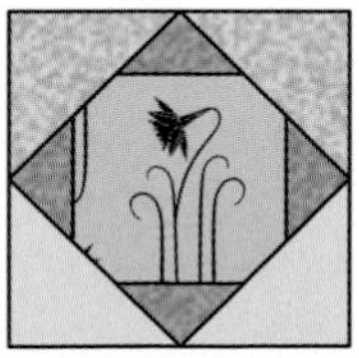

G57
2" x 2"
Make 1.

G57
2" x 2"
Make 1.

G57
2" x 2"
Make 1.

G57
2" x 2"
Make 1.

G57
1½" x 1½"
Make 4.

3. Make the pieced borders, placing fabrics as shown.

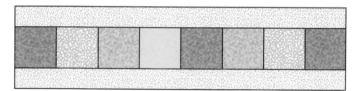

PB11
Make 4.

4. Sew the blocks into horizontal rows as shown. Join the rows.

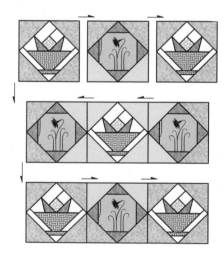

5. Sew pieced borders to the sides of the quilt top. Add a small Geometric block to each end of the remaining pieced borders, then sew them to the top and bottom edges.

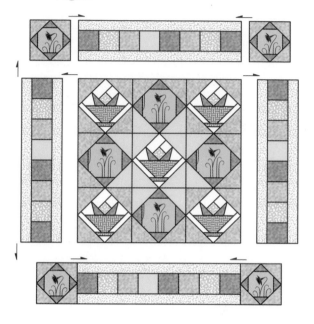

6. Sew 1½" x 9½" medium green border strips to the sides of the quilt top. Sew the remaining medium green border strips to the top and bottom edges.

7. Referring to "Finishing" on pages 90–94, layer your quilt top with batting and backing; baste. Quilt as desired and bind the edges.

Creative Option

You can use the same blocks to create a slightly different design. I substituted one of the light pink corner triangles in the large Geometric block for a light green triangle.

FINISHING

BATTING AND BACKING

Choose a very low-loft polyester or cotton batting. Hobbs Thermore, which is polyester, is a good choice. If you want to use cotton batting, choose one that doesn't require stitching at close intervals. Quilting intervals vary from ¼" to 10", depending on the brand and type of batting.

Cut the backing fabric and batting a few inches larger than the quilt top. Layer the backing, batting, and quilt top. If hand quilting, baste the three layers together with a long needle and light-colored thread. Start in the middle and work toward the outer edge. If machine quilting, pin-baste with small rust-proof pins. Place the pins in areas you do not intend to quilt.

◆ TIP ◆

I found that lightly pressing the quilt top and the backing to the cotton batting made the three layers stick together while I basted.

◆ ◆ ◆

SELECTING A QUILTING DESIGN

When considering how to quilt your miniature, keep in mind that you don't have a lot of space. Traditional hand quilting can be a little overwhelming in small patchwork. With seams so close together, it's also difficult to do. I think machine quilting is a better choice for these quilts, except in large, open areas where you can feature hand quilting.

In open areas, such as the middle of a Snowball block, you can feature a simple miniature design. In "Tulip and Spools" (page 75), I machine quilted a heart, then stipple quilted inside it. For most of the quilts, I either quilted in-the-ditch, outline quilted along blocks and border seams, or stipple quilted small areas. I even used a few fancy stitches on my machine in two borders. See "Jeweled Fans" (page 69) and "Flower Trellis" (page 72). You can also quilt around motifs in the fabric without marking quilting lines. The important thing to remember when it comes to quilting miniatures is that less is more.

QUILTING BY HAND

Use quilting thread that matches the fabric; the detail of each stitch won't be noticeable, but the overall design will. If you plan to switch colors often, use a small multicolor print for the backing; the change in thread color won't be as evident.

Since the quilts are so small, they make perfect take-along projects to quilt on the go.

QUILTING BY MACHINE

Even if you usually hand quilt your projects, let me encourage you to try machine quilting some of your miniatures. Their size makes them easy to manipulate under the needle. I am primarily a hand quilter, but I found that machine quilting miniatures was great fun.

You can straight-line quilt using a walking foot or free-form quilt using a darning foot. The walking foot feeds the layers through at the same rate. The darning foot allows you to move the quilt under the needle as if you were drawing with the needle. Free-form quilting takes a bit of practice. If you are inexperienced at machine quilting, experiment with the machine quilting needles and threads on a sample quilt sandwich before you begin your project. Make your sample using the same materials you used in your project.

If your machine makes decorative stitches, experiment with them. You may find the perfect stitch for a small border design. See "Machine-Made Quilting Designs" on the facing page for an example.

BINDING

A narrow binding works best for miniature quilts. I cut strips 1¾" wide for a double-fold binding. The finished width of the binding is ¼".

1. Machine baste around the perimeter of the quilt, ⅛" from the outer edge. Trim the batting and backing even with the quilt top.
2. If your 1¾"-wide binding strip isn't long enough to go around all the way around your quilt, join the ends of two strips at a 45° angle. Trim the excess fabric and press the seam open. Clip the "dog ears."

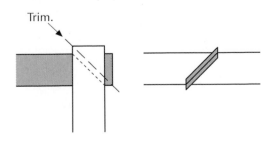

Trim.

Machine-Made Quilting Designs

Ginny Guaraldi, the maker of "Simply Spools" (page 75), shared a neat trick she does on her Bernina sewing machine. She selected a decorative stitch and stitched four single patterns, rotating each one ninety degrees. It produced a wonderful miniature-scale design. If your machine makes decorative stitches, follow the directions below to create your own quilting designs.

1. Select the stitch pattern.
2. Select mirror image (right-left) if you want the design to face a different direction.
3. Select the single-pattern function.
4. Select the secure-stitch button (if available on your machine). This secures the beginning stitches.
5. Begin the first pattern. Halfway through, disengage the secure-stitch button (if applicable).
6. When the pattern ends, pivot the quilt under the needle 90° and stitch the pattern again.
7. Repeat this procedure until you are stitching the fourth pattern. Halfway through the last pattern, select the secure stitch button again (if applicable).

I played with stitches on my Bernina and discovered several potential quilting designs.

These are the selected patterns.

This is how they appear when pivoted at 90°.

3. Place the binding strip wrong side up on the cutting mat. Place the 45-angle line on the rotary ruler along the straight edge of the strip near one end. Draw a "cutting line." Turn the strip and draw two more lines, each ¼" from the previous line. The first line is the cutting line, the second is the "sewing line" and the third is the "measuring line." Cut on the cutting line.

Mark the cutting line.

45°-angle line

Mark two more lines ¼" from the cutting line.

Cutting line
Measuring line
Sewing line

Cut on the cutting line.

4. Fold the strip in half lengthwise, wrong sides together, and press.

5. Place the binding on the front of the quilt in the middle of the bottom, lining up the raw edges of the binding with the raw edges of the quilt. Using a walking foot, sew the binding to the quilt with a ¼"-wide seam allowance; leave about 6" of binding loose so you can miter the beginning and ending of the binding later. Stop stitching ¼" from the corner of the quilt and backstitch.

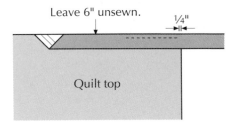

6. Turn the quilt to sew the next edge. Fold the binding up, away from the quilt, then down, even with the next side. The straight fold should be even with the upper edge of the quilt. Stitch from the edge to the next corner, stopping ¼" from the corner. Repeat for the remaining corners.

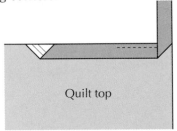

7. After the last corner is stitched, stop. Unfold the strip and place it under the beginning of the binding. Make a mark on the raw edge of the wrong side of the end strip to correspond with the measuring line on the beginning strip.

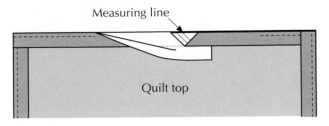

Measuring line

Quilt top

8. Place the 45°-angle line on the rotary ruler along the straight edge of the end tail, with the edge of the ruler at the mark. Draw a cutting line. Draw a sewing line ¼" away as shown. **Place the binding strip on the cutting table, away from the quilt, and cut on the cutting line.**

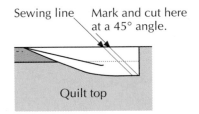

Sewing line   Mark and cut here at a 45° angle.

Quilt top

Wrong side of the binding strip

9. Pull the ends of the binding away from the quilt. Place the unfolded strips right sides together as shown. Pin, matching the 2 sewing lines, and stitch. Press the seam allowances open. Clip the "dog ears" and lightly press the strip in half again.

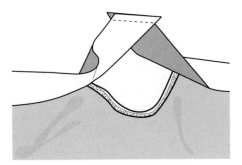

10. Return the strip to the edge of the quilt and finish the seam.

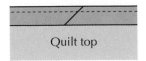

Quilt top

11. Fold the binding to the back, over the raw edges of the quilt. The folded edge of the binding should cover the machine-stitching lines. Blindstitch the binding in place.

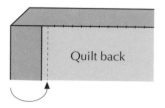 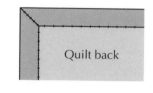

ADDING A SLEEVE

To hang your quilt on a wall, add a sleeve to the back.

1. Use the same fabric you used for the quilt backing. Cut a strip of fabric 6" wide and 1" narrower than the width of the quilt. Press each short end of the strip ¼" toward the wrong side twice, then hem.

2. With wrong sides together, sew the long sides of the strip together. Center the seam in the middle and press the center seam open.

Stitch wrong sides together.

Center seam and press open.

3. Pin the sleeve in place on the back of the quilt at the upper edge, with the seam toward the backing. Blindstitch the upper fold to the binding, then blindstitch the other fold to the back of the quilt. Do not stitch through to the front of the quilt.

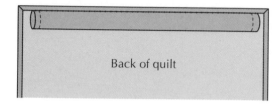

Back of quilt

SIGNING YOUR MINIATURE

It's important to add a label to your quilt to identify you as the maker. You can also add other important information, such as the date, the city and state where you live, the name of the quilt, and for whom the quilt was made if it was a gift. I use the following paper-pieced design for my miniature-quilt labels.

1. Trace the following design on a piece of paper, or make a photocopy. Cut the design out on the line, *not* ⅜" beyond the line as with the quilt block designs.

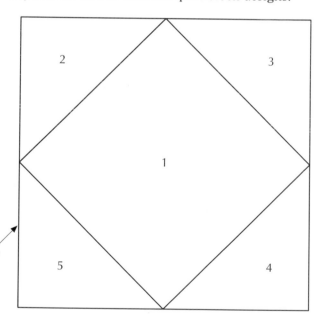

Cut on the line.

3" Foundation Design for Label

2. Paper piece the block, using a light fabric in the center that you can write on with a fine-point permanent pen.

3. When the block is complete, trim the fabric ⅜" from the edge of the paper and press the fabric over the outside edge to crease it. If you made a photocopy, don't touch the back of the foundation with the iron; the ink may smear and get on your iron.

4. Decide whether to place the label straight or on point on the back of the quilt. Write your message with a permanent pen. Remove the paper and attach it to the back of the quilt with a blind stitch.

QUILT TRIVIA

Just in case you've wondered how many pieces are in each quilt, I compiled this trivia chart. The total for each quilt is for the foundation pieces only. All the quilts are easy to make. It's just that some of them take a bit more time to complete because there are more pieces. In some instances, I was surprised that the number of pieces was higher for quilts that I thought went faster, and lower for quilts that I thought took more time. If you are enjoying yourself, the time goes by quickly.

Quilt	Total No. Pieces
Amish Baskets (page 73)	160
Simply Solids (page 80)	168
Country Baskets (page 77)	192
Mariner's Compass (page 66)	232
Tree of Life Medallion (page 79)	249
Simply Spools (page 75)	265
Scrap Hearts (page 71)	308
Little Nosegays (page 68)	320
Shade Trees (page 78)	333
Jeweled Fans (page 69)	352
Flower Trellis (page 72)	363
Log Cabin Garden (page 74)	368
Tulips & Spools (page 75)	369
My Little Town (page 70)	394
Rain Bonnet Sue (page 76)	418
Scrap Stars (page 65)	436
Spinning Stars (page 67)	472
GRAND TOTAL FOR ALL QUILTS	**5,399**

RESOURCE LIST

Contact the following suppliers and manufacturers regarding products suggested in this book.

Proportional Scale
The C-Thru Ruler Company
6 Britton Drive
Box 356
Bloomfield, Connecticut 06002

Add-An-Eighth Ruler
CM Designs
10669 Singleleaf Court
Parker, Colorado 80134

Foundation Papers for Use with *Easy Paper-Pieced Miniatures*
Martingale & Company
PO Box 118
Bothell, WA 98041-0118 USA
1-800-426-3126
Retail price $8.95

Other books by Carol Doak
Check your local quilt shop for these titles.
- *Easy Machine Paper Piecing*
- *Easy Mix & Match Machine Paper Piecing*
- *Easy Paper-Pieced Keepsake Quilts*
- *Easy Reversible Vests*
- *Show Me How to Paper Piece*
- *Your First Quilt Book (or it should be!)*

ABOUT THE AUTHOR

Carol Doak is an award-winning quiltmaker as well as a popular teacher and best-selling author. She has made more than one hundred fifty quilts since taking her first quiltmaking class in Worthington, Ohio. Carol began teaching beginning quiltmakers in 1980 through an adult-education quilting class and continued to teach this comprehensive class for several years in local quilt shops. She currently travels internationally to share her quiltmaking "Tricks of the Trade." Her lighthearted approach and ability to teach beginners as well as more advanced quilters have earned her high marks and positive comments from workshop participants wherever she travels.

Carol's blue-ribbon quilts have appeared in several books, including *Great American Quilts 1990* and *The Quilt Encyclopedia*, and on the covers of *Quilter's Newsletter Magazine, Quilt World, Quilting Today, McCall's Quilting,* and *Lady's Circle Patchwork Quilts.*

Carol's students encouraged her to write her first book in 1992. Since then, Carol has written eight more books and is working on another one!

Carol lives with her family in Windham, New Hampshire. She claims the cold winters give her plenty of reason to stockpile fabric, since it offers insulation as well as gratification.

PAPER-PIECING DESIGNS

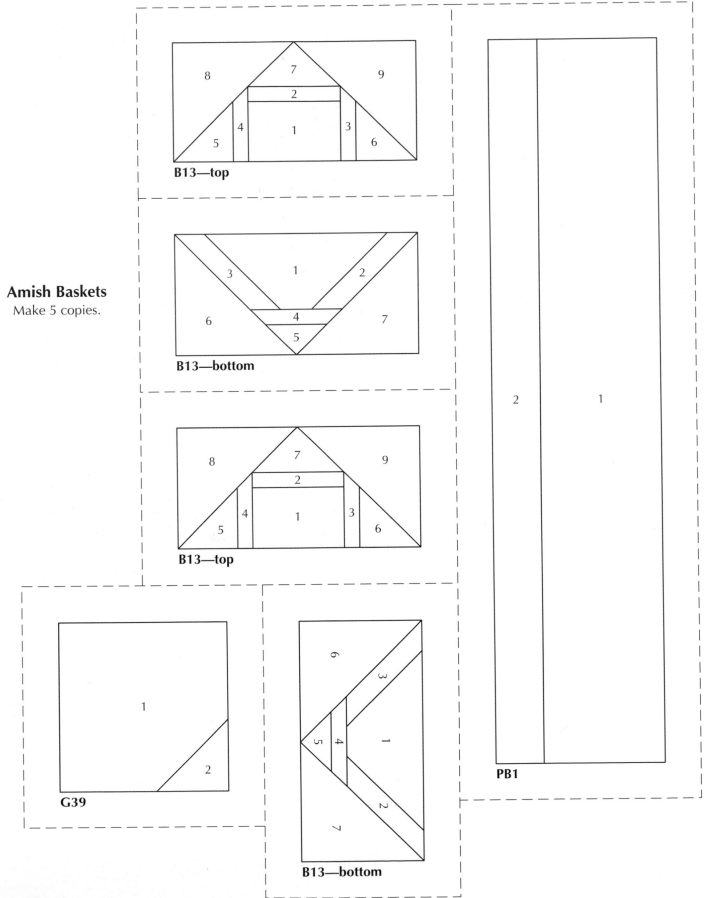

Amish Baskets

Make 5 copies.

B13—top

B13—bottom

B13—top

G39

B13—bottom

PB1

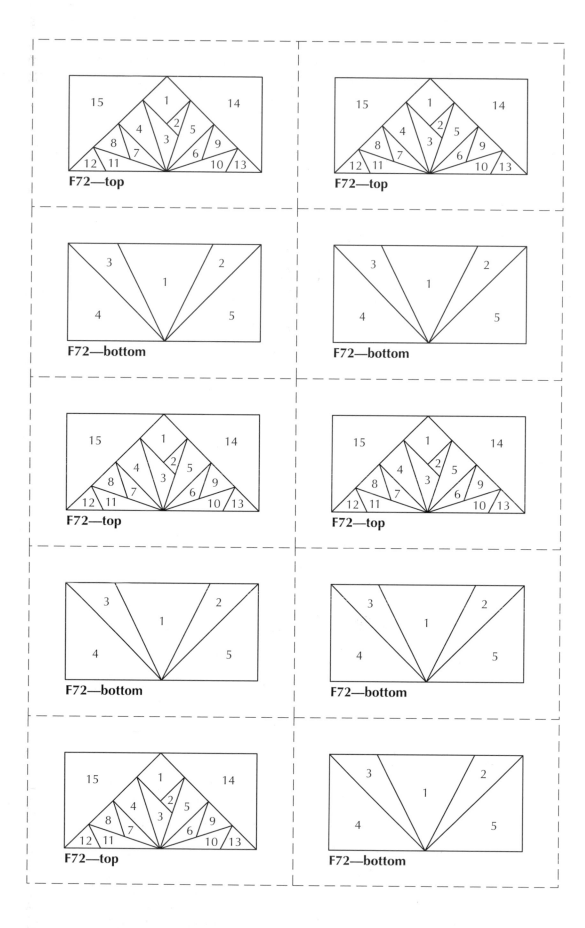

Little Nosegays
Make 4 copies.

Flower Trellis
Make 3 copies.

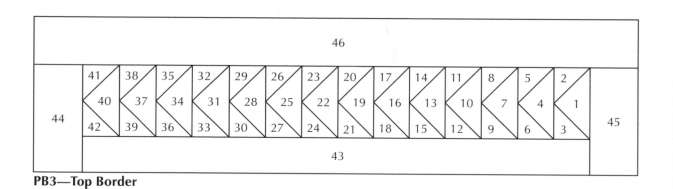

PB3—Top Border

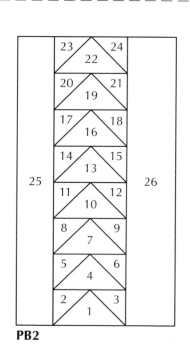

PB2

PB2

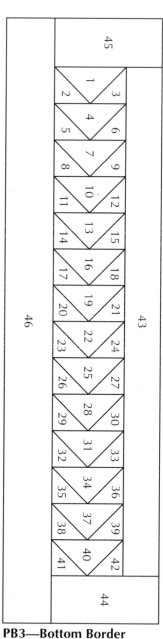

PB3—Bottom Border

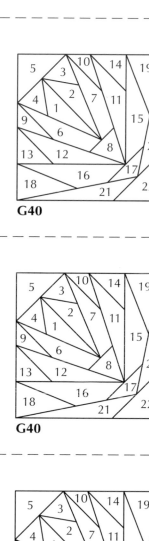

G40

G40

G40

Mariner's Compass
Make 2 copies.

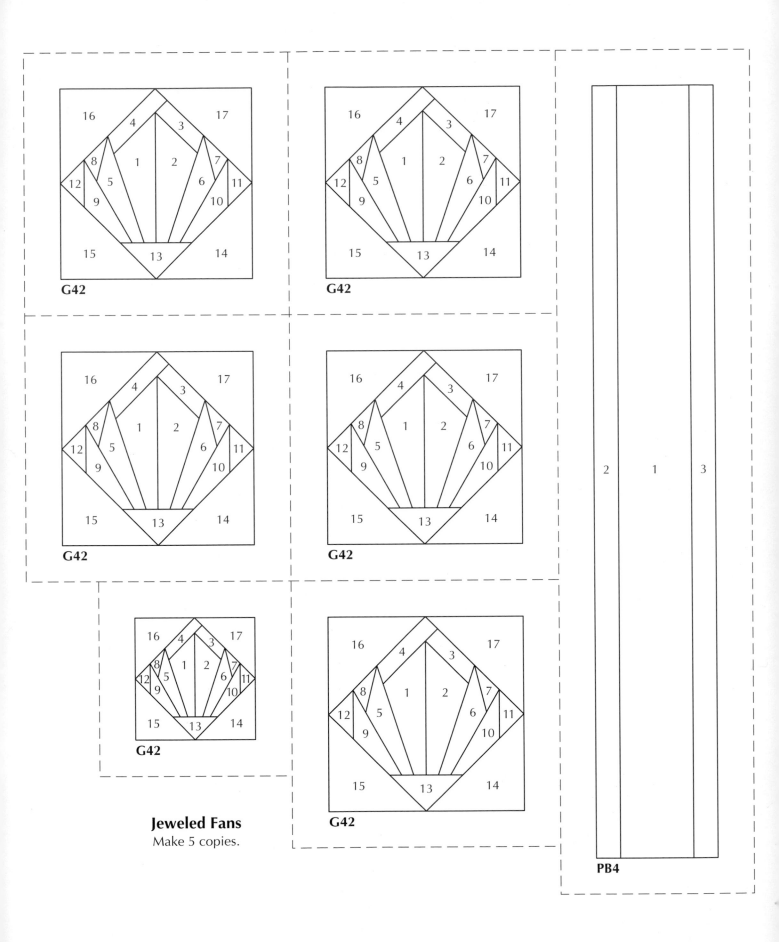

Jeweled Fans
Make 5 copies.

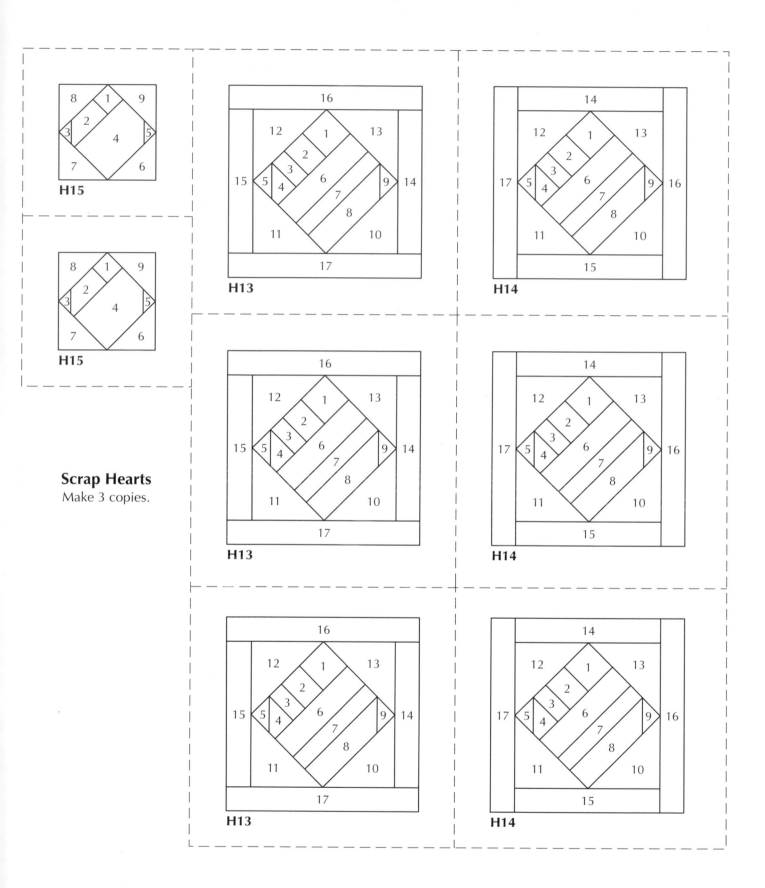

Scrap Hearts

Make 3 copies.

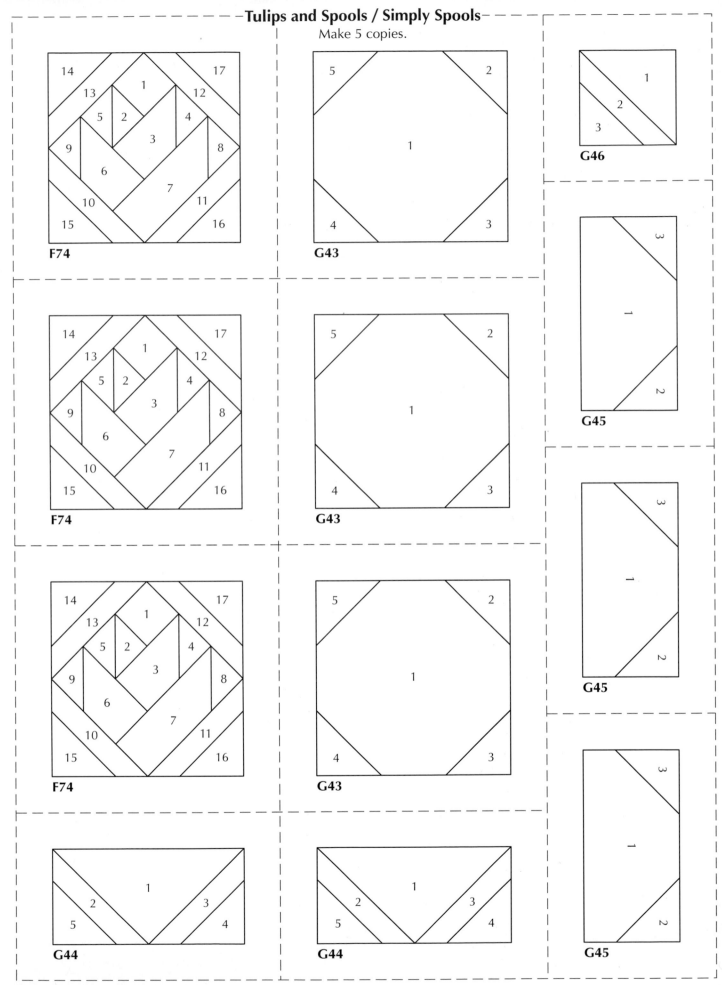

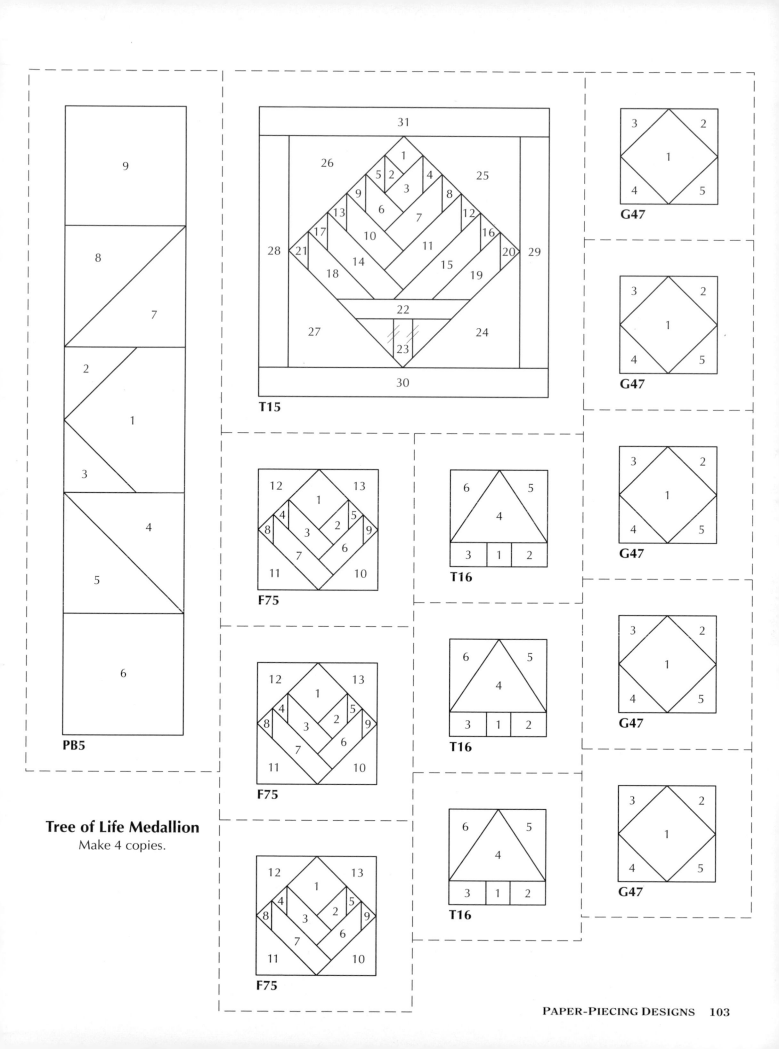

PB5

Tree of Life Medallion
Make 4 copies.

T15

F75

F75

F75

T16

T16

T16

G47

G47

G47

G47

G47

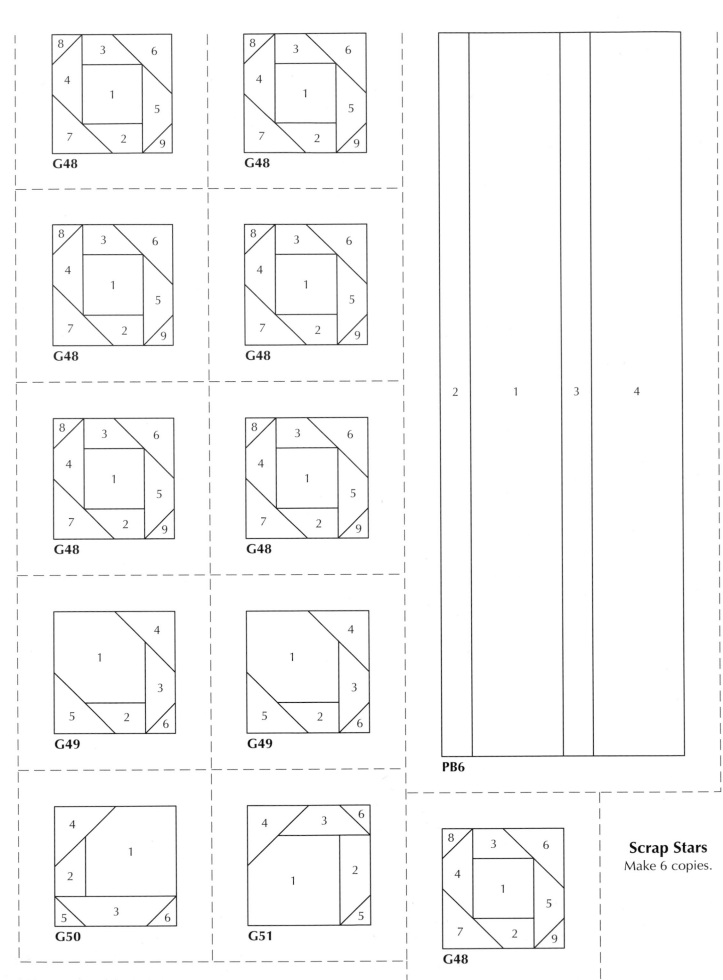

Scrap Stars
Make 6 copies.

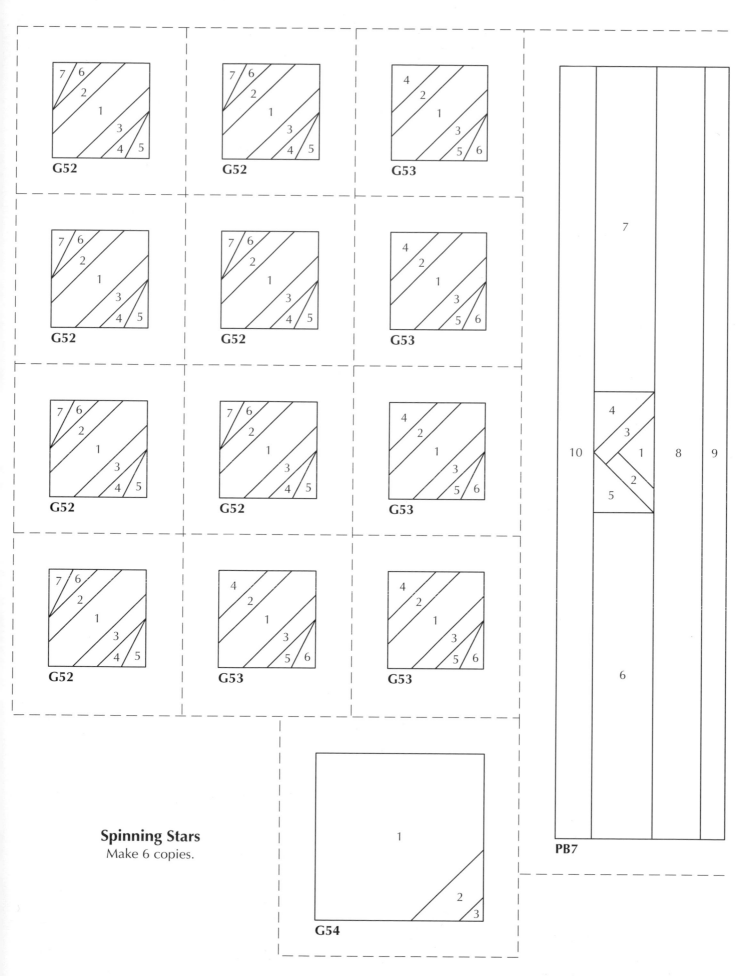

Spinning Stars
Make 6 copies.

My Little Town
Make 5 copies.

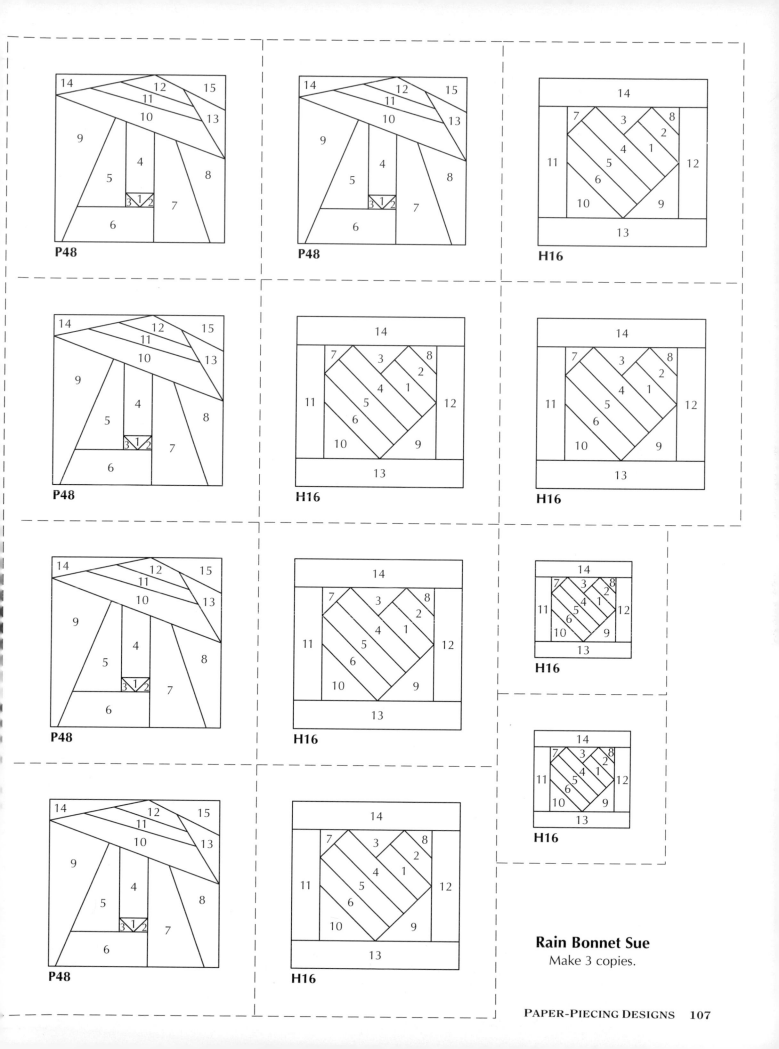

Rain Bonnet Sue
Make 3 copies.

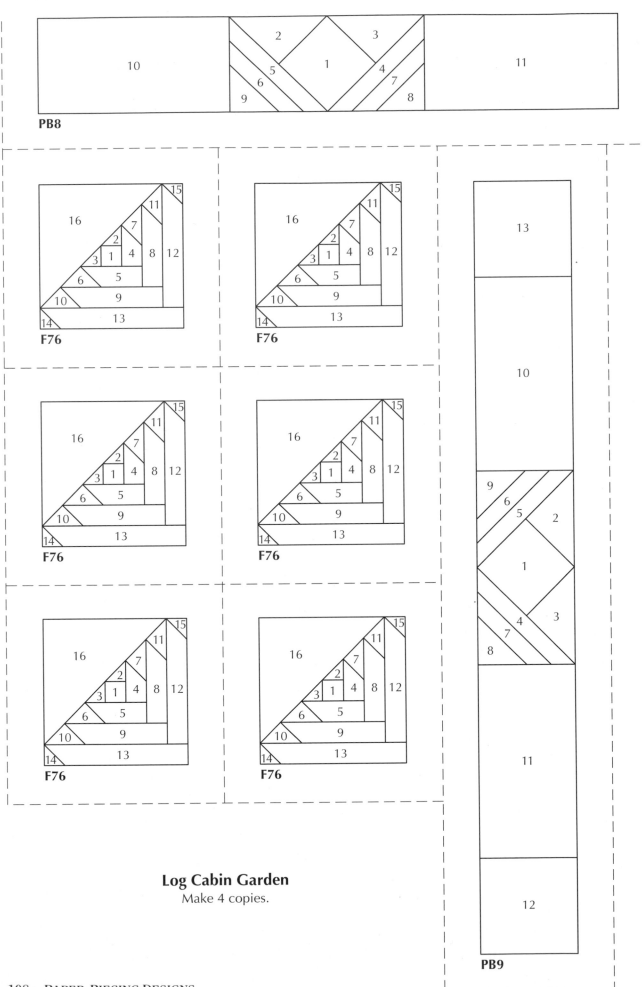

Log Cabin Garden

Make 4 copies.

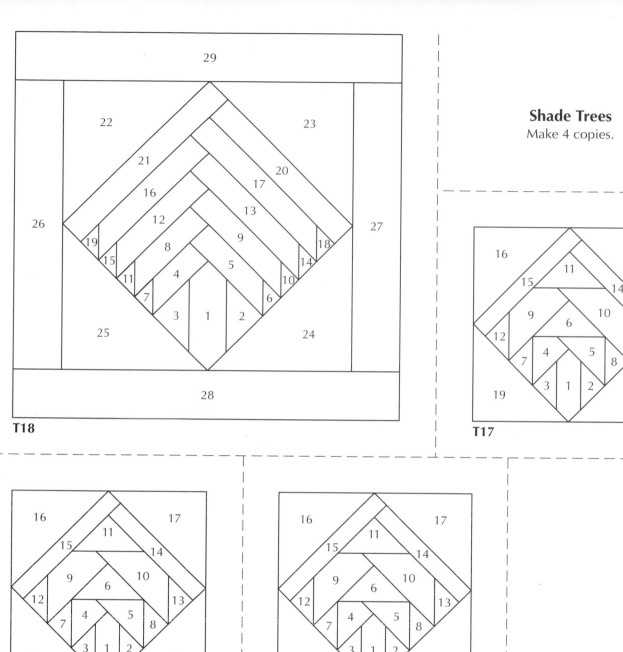

Shade Trees
Make 4 copies.

T18

T17

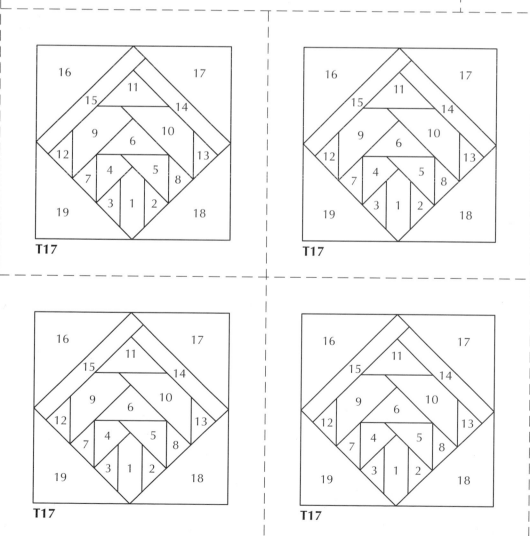

T17

T17

T17

T17

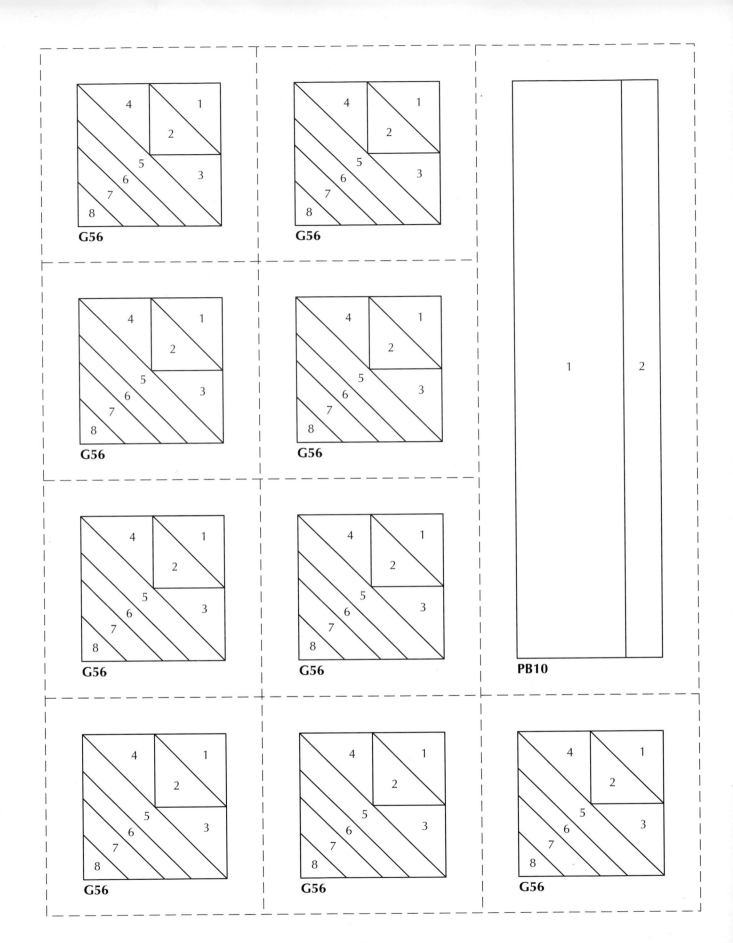

Simply Solids
Make 4 copies.

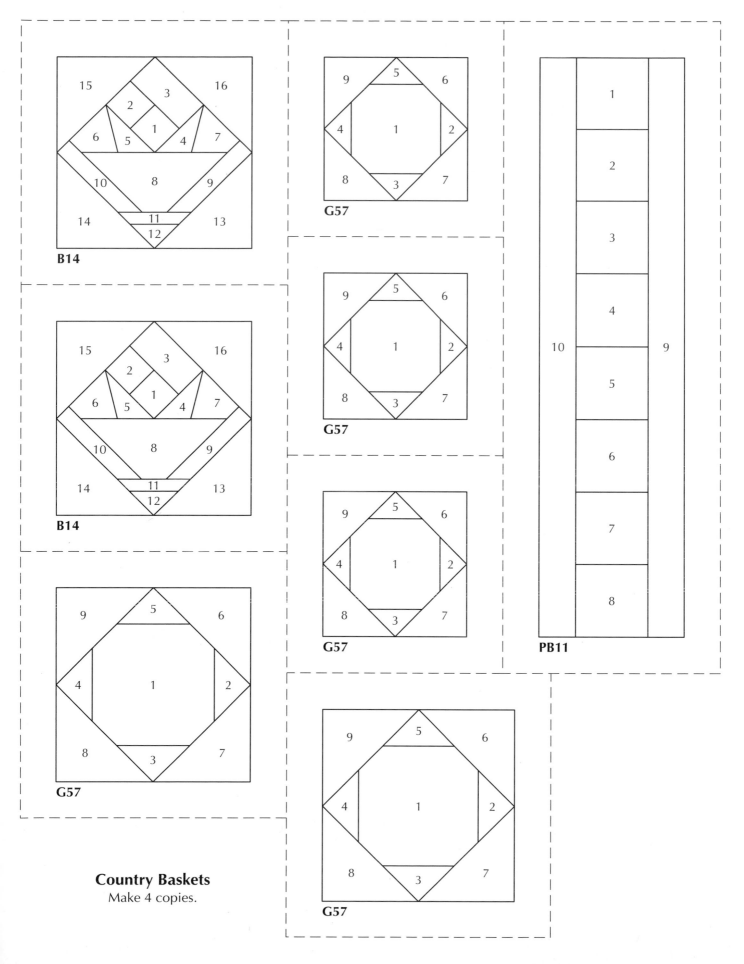

Country Baskets
Make 4 copies.

Publications and Products

Many titles are available at your local quilt shop.
For more information, write for a free color catalog
to Martingale & Company, PO Box 118, Bothell,
WA 98041-0118 USA.

☎ U.S. and Canada, call **1-800-426-3126** for the
name and location of the quilt shop nearest you.
Int'l: 1-425-483-3313   **Fax:** 1-425-486-7596
E-mail: info@patchwork.com
Web: www.patchwork.com

3.98